Find Your Seasoning
Find Yourself

☑ Parsley ☐ Pepper ☐ Garlic ☐ Ginger

Woody Yarrow   "Hey You"

JV Football 4;   Wrestling Manager 3;
Cross Country Manager 2;   Optimo Service
Club 2;   Intramurals 3;   School Store 2, 3,
4;   Choir 2, 3;   Future Librarians 4.
GOAL: To have my own subscription to
        National Geographic

☑ Parsley ☐ Pepper ☐ Garlic ☐ Ginger

Grindelia Clary   "Pinky"

Kitchen Bouquet Award Winner 3, Second-place
"New Uses for Swiss Miss Chocolate
Pudding" Contest 4;   VESTA Service Club
Handmaiden 2;   Franklin Library Country-
Thimble-of-the-Month Club 2, 3, 4.
GOAL: To have my own sewing machine

☐ Parsley ☑ Pepper ☐ Garlic ☐ Ginger

Alexanders Ginseng

"Fast Track"
Varsity Debate Team 2, 3, Captain 4;
Yacht Club 3;   Polo Club 4;   School Store
Designer Merchandise Buyer 4;   Morning
Intercom Announcements Moderator 4;
Future Physicians, 2, 3, 4;   Future Lawyers
2, 3, 4;   Future Scientists 2, 3, 4;   Future
C.P.A.'s 2, 3, 4.
GOAL: To know Gstaad like the back of
        my hand

☐ Parsley ☐ Pepper ☑ Garlic ☐ Ginger

Erica Comfrey *"Rhythm Master"*
Drama Club Costume Coordinator, "Oh Calcutta" 4; Cheerleader 4; Powderpuff Football 4; Field Hockey Intramurals 2, 3, 4; "Miss Popularity" 4; 4-H, Poultry Division, 2; Kayak Club 4.
GOAL: To experience it all and have a BLAST!

☐ Parsley ☐ Pepper ☐ Garlic ☑ Ginger

Poke Liverwort *"Chip"*
Chess Club Pawn 2, Knight 3, Bishop 4; Mensa Futurists, Junior Division 2, 3, Historian 4; National Honor Society 4; Young Republicans 2; Rare Stamp and Coin Club 3; Computer Science Club 4.
GOAL: To have my own home computer to monitor my cashflow automatically.

☐ Parsley ☐ Pepper ☐ Garlic ☑ Ginger

Myrtle Linseed *"Myrt"*
Gertrude Stein Literary Club 2, 3; Barbara Pym Scholarship Winner 4; Principal's Committee on Hall Pass Procedures 4;
GOAL: I wish that every American could share in the wealth and resources of this land, free of limits and free to be themselves. I will work to serve this ideal.

☐ Parsley ☐ Pepper ☑ Garlic ☐ Ginger

Herb Snakeroot *"Nads"*
JV Football 2; Varsity Football 3, 4; Wrestling 2, 3; Science Club 2, Project: "Distillates from corn and grain"; Bumper Sticker Committee 3, 4; Auto Club 2;
GOAL: I want to ride the big ones in Hawaii before I die.

Find your Seasoning Find yourself

Your Ultimate Guide to Riches, Sex, Diet and Success.

☐ Parsley ☑ Pepper ☐ Garlic ☐ Ginger

Angelica Hellebore *"Angelica"*

Latin Honor Society Banquet Menu
Assignments Director 4;   STELLAE Service
Club 2, Vice-President 3, President 4;
Sadie Hawkins Dance Decorations
Coordinator 4;   Pep Rally Seating
Assignments Committee Head 3, 4;
Sophomore Play "Hello Dolly" (Dolly) 2;
Junior Play "Mame" (Mame) 3;   Senior Play
"MacBeth" (MacBeth) 4.
*GOAL: To be a personal friend of Prince
Charles and H.R.H. Diana*

By Hickey & Hughes

(Robert Hickey, Hp.D.)
(Kathleen Hughes, Hp.D.)

(Illustrations by Robert Hickey, Hp.D.)

ACROPOLIS BOOKS LTD.
WASHINGTON, D.C.

Dedication

To
Al Hackl,
for everything

Acknowledgments

We are indebted to so many people, it is difficult to know where to begin.

Thanks particularly to our families and friends, whose spiciness, suggestions, love, and patience kept us cooking: to Neil, Jenny and Sara, Kay Pope, George and Marie Norris, Georgia and Mark Rolewski, Carolyn and Rick Edwards, Julianne and Mike Cline, and Veronica Pickman.

To Mr. and Mrs. Thomas J. Hickey, Bruce Radford, Jane Ann Simpson, Carol Sudol, Mary Hickey, Anka Kroc, Tom Hickey, Lisa Caruthers, Sandra Seymour, Ivan Franceus, Wear Culvahouse, Bill Gallagher, Al and Judy Eichner, Ben Killebrew, Jane King, Michael Roussell, D. J. and Bob Thompson, Harold Thompson, Anne and Bob Neville, Howard Millard, Jim and Alice Shisler, and Lee and Lillian Goodman.

And heartfelt thanks to the wonderful staff (present and past) at Acropolis, whose friendship is a great source of strength— especially to Al Hackl, Laurie Tag, Nancy Brandwein, Jennifer Prost, Sandy and Phil Trupp, John Hackl, Muriel Hackl, David Uslan, Chris Jones, Eileen Tansill, Colleen Holmes, Laurie Richardson, Sharon Smith, Irma Gallagher, and all the others who make a day of work, fun.

To Barbara Hendra, Rosemary Hickey, and Sybille Millard for their special efforts.

Thanks to the authors of dozens of how-to and self-help books, we worked with at Acropolis Books. If it were not for Carole Jackson, Ruthanne Olds, Dean Hummel and Carl McDaniels, Janet Wallach, Leatrice Eiseman, Joanne Lemieux, and Clare Miller, the Science of Herbopsychiatry might never have been conceived. Thanks to every author at Acropolis who has ever thanked either of us by name in their book. The gesture was always appreciated.

Thanks to the hundreds of people at parties who willingly took our test, found their Seasoning, and laughed with us.

And, last of all, we want to thank *YOU*, for buying this book and reading this far.

ACROPOLIS BOOKS, LTD.
Colortone Building. 2400 17th St. N.W.
Washington, D.C. 20009

Printed in the United States of America by
COLORTONE PRESS
Creative Graphics, Inc.
Washington, D.C. 20009

Attention: Schools and Corporations
ACROPOLIS books are available at quantity discounts with bulk purchase for educational, business, or sales promotional use. For information, please write to: SPECIAL SALES DEPARTMENT, ACROPOLIS BOOKS, LTD., 2400 17th ST., N.W. WASHINGTON, D.C. 20009

Are there Acropolis Books you want
but cannot find in your local stores?
You can get any Acropolis book title in print. Simply send title and retail price, plus 50 cents per copy to cover mailing and handling costs for each book desired. District of Columbia residents add applicable sales tax. Enclose check or money order only, no cash please, to: ACROPOLIS BOOKS LTD. 2400 17th St. N.W. WASHINGTON, D.C. 20009

Library of Congress Cataloging in Publication Data
Hickey, Robert.
    Find your seasoning, find yourself.
    Includes index.
    1. Success—Anecdotes, facetiae, satire, etc.
2. Personality tests—Anecdotes, facetiae, satire, etc.
3. Herbs—Psychological aspects—Anecdotes, facetiae, satire, etc. I. Hughes, Kathleen,. II. Title.
BF637.S8H47 1984 158 .1'0207 84-14487 ISBN O-87491-759-X (alk. paper)

First Printing: September 1984

I knew I was a WINTER. But I never suspected I was a PARSLEY.

For years now I've been appearing on television and before large groups to tell people about the *Color Me Beautiful* concepts. But somehow, I've never gotten used to all the attention and glamour. I'd really rather stay quietly at home with my children. This had gotten to be quite a problem, especially since I have a new book, *Color for Men,* to promote.

So I decided to consult my old friends, Kathleen Hughes and Robert Hickey, who had been so helpful to me in the publishing of *Color Me Beautiful.* I knew they were clever but I didn't know they were herbo-psychiatrists.

They gave me *The Test* from *Find Your Seasoning, Find Yourself.* I discovered I was a fresh, tender, traditional PARSLEY with GARLIC undertones. No wonder I get nervous away from home!

Hickey and Hughes suggested I dig into my herbal personality syndrome and pull out my PEPPER traits. I found I do have a "pinch" of the fiery and dramatic in me. Now I can be a PEPPER in public and a quiet Parsley at home.

I highly recommend *Find Your Seasoning.* You really will *Find Yourself.* And you'll laugh all the time you are doing it.

—**Carole Jackson**
Author
Color Me Beautiful

Contents

So many fascinating considerations fall under the brim of herbopsychiatry.

Parsley...Pepper...Garlic...or Ginger
Which is your Seasoning?

Chapter One

Your Flavor In The Great Stew of Life

"Grasses and herbs which grow upon the mountains hath been given particular signatures where man may read in ledgible characters.**"**

William Coles
The Doctrine of Signatures

Change Your Life Right This Second
At last...here is your simple, easy-to-use, short guide to improving every aspect of your life—your sex life, your monetary value, your looks, your job...*everything.*

"What Is this System, and How Can I Get Started?
All you have to do is find out whether YOU are a Parsley, Pepper, Garlic or Ginger, and you'll be ready to start cooking.

"But How?" You Implore
Through the amazing new science of *herbopsychiatry*, described here for the first time ever. Recently unearthed after years of study by your authors, herbopsychiatry is a revolutionary self-help system that reduces the entire spectrum of complex human behavior to four simple categories. As soon as you understand the categories, you can understand LIFE, everyone else, and yourself.

The Secret
The secret, we've found, is in the Seasonings. For, just as Nature has four distinct herbal groups (leaves, fruits, bulbs and roots) so,

we prove, there are four herbopsychiatric personality types that correspond to Nature: *Parsleys, Peppers, Garlics and Gingers.*

- *Parsleys* are the crisp, fresh, quiet people, tender but strong, the traditionalists you can count on.
- *Peppers* are those fiery, sensuous, attention-demanding people, complex, sophisticated and too hot, unless you take just a pinch of them.
- *Garlics* are ripe, generous, earthy, and fun-loving people, reeking of life.
- *Gingers* are those dramatic but mysterious individuals inclined to be biting, but rich in subtle flavor.

YOU are one of these exciting herbal personalities. And, once you know what your Seasoning is, your life will be changed. You'll be able to flavor and savor the Great Stew of Life!

Herbopsychiatry — The Missing Link

Herbopsychiatric Quadrant	Herbopersonality Spectrum
The Family of Leaves	Parsleys
The Family of Fruits	Peppers
The Family of Bulbs	Garlics
The Family of Roots	Gingers

This chart demonstrates the link between Nature's herbal families and the personality spectrums of human beings.

It's Easy

Now without a Ph.D. in psychology, just a basic understanding of herbopsychiatry, you can permeate LIFE...and find harmony with the rest of the world's population. Herbopsychiatry promises to...

- give you your own identity *instantly* (no waiting for complicated test results);
- allow you to judge other people *immediately;*
- help you solve the *real* problems of life, like how to be RICHER, SEXIER, THINNER, and MORE SUCCESSFUL.

Get Started Now!

Just read this comprehensive guide to life. It's all RIGHT here in these pages. It has worked for others and now it can work for you. Everything in the herbopsychiatric approach to life has been thoroughly people-tested.

Rave Reviews!

Hear what others who've applied this system to their previously tawdry existences say now...

> **"**For years, I would watch the 'Lawrence Welk Show' only after carrying the portable TV into the laundry room. I was embarrassed because friends who watched the educational channel said my show wasn't 'high culture.' Now that Hickey and Hughes have shown me my Seasoning, I don't care what others say. I'm out of the laundry room and into my new life as a full-leafed Parsley! Now I can say to the world, 'Norma Zimmer, I love you.**"**
>
> **Tansy Carum, Garden City, NY**

> **"**I was trying to be Florence Nightingale twenty-four hours a day. I was miserable in my starched white nurse's uniform, helping other people all day. Now I've found myself in Pepperdom. After work, I let myself sizzle in turquoise boots, sequin

A sweet Parsley place, filled with the gentle floral motifs Parsley people thrive among.

Pepper pizazz on display from the preposterous hippo cigarette holder to the mirrored mat...never a solemn moment.

jeans, and a fiery halter top. Now I can stand my uniform during the day because I have the promise of the REAL me at night. And, I wear red panties under that uniform—or, if I'm in the mood, none at all. I'm also taking acting lessons at the YWCA. **99**

Viola Heartsease, Stillwater, KS

66My wife called me 'anal compulsive.' That's not a very nice name for one who dislikes bathroom talk as much as I do. After Hickey and Hughes did my Seasoning for me, I discovered that, as a Ginger, it's natural to cut the fat off of bacon and the seeds out of my bananas. My guilt is gone!**99**

Orris Pigeonberry, Garden Grove, CA

66My astrologer said I was a Scorpio. That meant I was a disagreeable insect. The Chinese told me I was born in the Year of the Pig, but I'm Jewish. Biorhythms had me labeled as a Morning Person, but I work nights. At last, I found Hickey and Hughes. They pronounced me a Garlic, and it's okay for me to like pizza, beer and sit-coms. This I can identify with happily. **99**

Bowman Root, Humus, NH

Let's Spice Up Your Life!

Now you find your Seasoning and find yourself. Take the Test in the first chapter and get cooking in the Great Stew of Life.

A tasteful Ginger table ensemble emphasizes the quality, order and style demanded by Ginger people.

A bountiful Garlic place setting complete with the beverages, clutter and informality Garlic people like best.

Chapter Two

Put Spice In Your Life: THE TEST

Find Your Seasoning...Find Yourself

Now comes the fun—finding your Seasoning. Once you've discovered whether you are a Parsley, Pepper, Garlic, or Ginger, you'll be able to choose the right diet, dinner partner, lover, wardrobe, makeup, hair color, job, image, pet, house, furniture, and furniture polish. Sound simple-minded? It is. So...just relax and discover your Seasoning soul.

The Test

STEP 1: ELEVEN QUESTIONS TO DETERMINE YOUR SEASONING

Take a long look at yourself in a short mirror, near natural daylight if possible. Look at your skin, hair, and eyes. Decide what colors they are. Then, look into your soul and answer the following questions.

1. Which is the list of names from which you would name your pet?

   A. Spot, Nana, Fido, Blackie, Dog, Kitty, Bambi, Pinky, Maisie, Cindy

   B. Glorious, Chi Chi, Vesuvius, Godzilla, Lana, Temptation, Roman Ruin, Urbanity, Tiffany

   C. Sophia, McIntosh, Luciano, Olivia, Devil, Don Juan, Thunder, Boomer, Wiener, Cattywumpus

   D. Nefertiti, Anise, Scrooge, Leonard, Solemnity, Oedipus, Prince, Pagan, Ariadne, Thalia, Bell Jar, Prufrock

2. Your four best friends give you a surprise birthday party, complete with presents. Which are likely to be yours?

   A. egg poacher, wool gloves, stationery, picture album, hedge clippers

   B. linen cocktail napkins for forty, rhumba record, tap shoes, *Town & Country* magazine, neon jogging suit, pasta machine

   C. pizza warmer, whoopee cushion, six pack of beer, stadium blanket, colorful tee shirt with "I like Ike" on it

   D. classic leather belt, insulting birthday card, bottle of wine of an excellent vintage

3. If you could live at any time, which time would it be?

   A. In a time of peace, in a beautifully landscaped suburb, without crime or pollution. Morals are defined, clothes classic, and being a little bit square is all right, where people stay close to home with their families, and their major concerns are the upcoming State Fair, the picnic on Saturday, and good clean fun.

   B. In a time of prosperity, a recovery after a great war with new, sophisticated music, high fashion, dramatic romance, and dancing 'till dawn. Fast cars, outrageous things to try—an energetic age.

   C. In a time of innocence, in the Garden of Eden before Eve bit into the apple. Fruit is at finger's reach and fish leap happily over the waves. Sun, sand, and sensuous pleasures abound.

   D. In a time of reason in a great and noble city. People of superior intellect are the heroes. The air is electric with new ideas. Exhibitions, openings, and brilliant debates are all part of the normal excitement of the day.

4. You've been invited to a costume party. How would you go about finding a costume?

   A. Put together something from vacation souvenirs in your closet, such as Mexican hat and castanets; or squeeze into your old Girl Scout or Navy uniform; or raid the Goodwill bag and come as a bum or gypsy

   B. Search out the most exquisite ingredients for a famous person costume, and go as Carmen Miranda, Scarlet

O'Hara, Wonder Woman, Prince Charles, Rhett Butler, bare-chested lion tamer

C. Go as Cupid, clown, Mae West, lifeguard, teddy bear, football player, cheerleader, Elvis Presley, Marilyn Monroe, or member of the opposite sex

D. Wear evening clothes if you have them, otherwise refuse to wear costume at all and just go dressed as you would to any party

5. You are walking in the woods one afternoon and come upon an old house. You go in, wander around, then return home. Which item would you most likely remember?

A. the old rocking chair on a faded rag rug

B. the sweeping staircase

C. the chipped figurine of a frolicking shepherd and his milkmaid friend

D. the beautiful hand-tooled leather walls in the library

6. Everywhere you go you add to a favorite collection. What would that collection be?

A. small figurines, Civil War bullets, thimbles, lemon juicers

B. dramatic ethnic jewelry, serving pieces, daring shoes, famous lovers

C. plants, throw pillows, beer cans, dolls, guppies, paper placemats, sugar packets

D. probably wouldn't collect anything, but, if you did, it might be pre-Colombian pottery, fountain pens, or stamps

7. If you could live anywhere you wanted, where would it be?

A. a lovely dignified town, or peaceful country place, renovated to a pristine version of its renowned history, gently caught in a moment of its past

B. a bright, showy place, full of exotic blossoms and people from around the globe. Classical and modern dance together in a celebration of dazzling excitement, glamour, and easy living

C. a big, warm, friendly place with lots of opportunities for meeting people and having fun

D. a sophisticated town, teeming with fascinating people, where you can lose yourself and never know anyone if you don't choose to

8. Choose the group which most clearly resembles your aspirations in life.

A. accountant, PTA member in good standing, librarian, genealogist, medical researcher, banker, bookkeeper, dietitian

B. diva, famous host or hostess, nightclub owner, matador, race car driver, renowned tap dancer

C. salesperson, social worker, missionary, masseur/masseuse, union organizer, waitress, urologist/gynocologist, emergency-room technician

D. poet, writer, pianist, artist, brain surgeon, tennis pro, inventor, recluse

9. You are stuck on a desert island. What would you do first?

A. seek shelter, find water, build a fire, befriend Gilligan

B. explore the island for hidden treasure

C. discard your clothes and ride on a giant turtle's back while blowing into a conch shell

D. try to build a raft to get off the island and back to civilization as quickly as possible

10. You have a chance to switch jobs for awhile. What would you do?

A. make sweet cream butter or plant a Colonial garden in an early-American arts demonstration

B. study with a famous designer or brilliant entrepreneur, go with her to the big exhibition and soak up the excitement as well as the contacts

C. teach body surfing and shell collecting to Head Start youngsters

D. rent a typewriter and a loft and write the Great American Novel

11. If you would be any character in the movie, "The Wizard of Oz," which would you be cast as?

   A. Glenda, the Good Witch of the North

   B. The Wicked Witch of the East

   C. The Tin Woodsman

   D. The Scarecrow

Scoring

O.K. Now add up all your As, Bs, Cs and Ds:

☐ A   ☐ B   ☐ C   ☐ D

Consider your totals. Then use either Method #1 or Method #2 to determine your true Seasoning.

Method #1 TO DETERMINE YOUR SEASONING

Take the square root of each score. Multiply this amount by the area of a circle nine inches in diameter. Recalling the Pythagorean Theorum, treat each amount as if it were degrees Centigrade and convert to degrees Farenheit. On metric graph paper, plot each number in the following manner:

- for every A quotient, go one up and one to the left;
- for every B quotient, go down one and to the right one;
- for every C quotient, go up one and to the right one;
- for every D quotient, go down one and to the left one.

If your result is in the top left quadrant, you are a Parsley.

If you are in the bottom right quadrant, you are a Pepper.

If you find yourself in the top right quadrant, you are a Garlic.

If you are situated in the bottom left quadrant, you can only be a Ginger.

Method #2 TO DETERMINE YOUR SEASONING

- If you got mostly As, you are a Parsley.
- If you got mostly Bs, you are a Pepper.
- If you got mostly Cs, you are a Garlic.
- If you got mostly Ds, you are a Ginger.

STEP 2: A DIFFERENT APPROACH TO DISCOVERING YOUR SEASONING

Now, blindfold yourself. Then go to the store and buy the freshest bunch of parsley, the most aromatic garlic, the sharpest ginger root or the one with the most unusual shape, and a big bright red pepper. Pay for them.

Take them home and place them in a row in front of you on the kitchen table or in your favorite spot in the house. Get rid of all distracting smells, e.g., Airwick Solid, kitty litter, visiting uncle's cigars.

A. Pick up each herb or spice (there is a difference) and *Smell*. Decide which smell is the most pleasing to you, which smell conjures up images of things you like. If you have a cold and can't smell, hold up each herb or spice next to your ear. Can you hear the ocean?

B. Taste each one. Which is the most pleasing to you?

C. Which one do you like best for texture and shape? Does it remind you of things you most like to touch...of the person you most like to touch, perhaps?

D. Take off your blindfold. Which color do you like the best?

Now, think over your sensuous reactions to each herb or spice. Which Seasoning did you choose most often? Which did you choose the least? Write your answer here:

Favorite _____

Least Favorite _____

Scoring

Did you like or dislike this part of the test? Mark you answer below:

☐ I loved it. It really felt good.
☐ I despised it. I thought it was utterly ridiculous.

What Your Score Means

If you didn't like this part of the test, chances are you are a Parsley or a Ginger. If you really enjoyed it, you are a Pepper or a Garlic. As to the relationship between your sensuous choice of an herb or spice and your true Seasoning, research is still ongoing at the Mayo Clinic.

The Test Results:

What If You Are Getting Mixed Seasonings?

If you still aren't sure of your Seasoning, answer these questions:

1. If you are deciding between

   - Parsley and Garlic
   - Ginger and Pepper
   - Garlic and Ginger   OR
   - Pepper and Parsley, *choose one:*

   A. I would rather stay home in front of a warm fire, with one special person and have a cozy dinner. Maybe we would listen to music, or read and retire early.

   B. I would much rather go to a big wing-ding, be with all sorts of great people, and PARTY. Dance, dance, dance, and go home only when I'm about to drop.

   If you chose A, then you are a Parsley or a Ginger.
   If you chose B, then you are a Pepper or a Garlic.

2. If you are deciding between Parsley and Ginger, consider what you would do in this situation:
   At the bus stop, a nicely dressed woman in obvious distress asks to borrow a dollar and says if you will give her your name and address, she'll mail you the money later.

   A. You give her the dollar, your name, and address. The amount is not the issue, and she seems the sort to return the money as she promises.

   B. You start to walk away, but then tell her she can probably find a Traveler's Aid office or a policeman somewhere nearby. You really don't want to become involved.

   If you answered A, you are a Parsley.
   If you answered B, you are a Ginger.

3. If you are deciding between Garlic and Pepper, ask yourself what you would do in this situation:
   At a large dinner party, you suddenly let out a loud, embarrassing body noise. You would...

   A. Laugh

   B. Pretend it was your dinner partner.

   If you answered A, you are a Garlic.
   If you answered B, you are a Pepper.

4. If you still can't decide, then you are a Bouquet Garni. (If you are from Baltimore, you may be an Old Bay Seasoning.)

Now, take your new Seasoning identity and discover all the new vistas opening before you in the next chapters....

Chapter Three

Purity and Virtue
PARSLEY

Parsley People

Parsley people are just like their herbal namesake...tender and fresh. Innocently open to the sun and rain, he's that quiet friend who is honestly thrilled at your good news. You may feel you should protect your Parsley friend. There he is, wide-eyed, fully anticipating gentle misty rains, followed by clear sunny skies.

Parsleys have very shallow roots and live in constant fear of being uprooted. Because of this, they feel at their most comfortable right in their own home. They do not travel well. Take them away from their own toilet and "comfy" bed, and they can't function.

Parsley is a fragile plant. Too little water and it wilts, too much and it rots. Parsleys thrive in average soil. Their skin is as tender as a new leaf. They are at their most delightful when absolutely fresh. She is your Doris Day, forever sweet, always about to break into, "Que Sera, Sera," never losing her virginity before marriage.

The Parsley man loves to sip his tea from Mother's china.
He appreciates it and takes good care of it.

Any impropriety she commits is an embarrassing mistake, and, somehow she escapes unscathed. She is the utltimate good girl, glamorous by mistake.

He is the grown-up altar boy, the smiling, clean-cut neighbor's kid. This is the man to ask for directions when lost in a strange city. He's the polished naval officer, the unathletic perpetual preppy. He can be sexy, in his stong, quiet way. Actually, women love to tempt him, knowing full well that he won't take advantage of them unless they really want to be tempted.

Parsley improves everything in the immediate vicinity, much like a potpourri of sweet petals. It's a freshener, a purifier, a garnish that dresses up the main course of Life. Never seeking to be the focal point, Parsleys ask YOU questions and make YOU feel interesting. They are really intrigued by where you buy your hamburger. They are *fascinated* to hear about your mother's sick aunt. They *long* to know why your big toe aches.

You rarely find a Parsley sprig off by itself. They come in bunches, wrapped neatly with a blue rubber band, and, in bunches, they have true power. They are genuine family people, really caring for and nurturing each other. They treat parenthood with the professionalism the rest reserve for careers, and their children are children no matter how ancient they become or what terrible crime they commit.

Parsleys are always a tasteful addition to any event, showing up appropriately dressed and on time. You think of them fondly afterwards, perhaps regretting you didn't pay them a little more attention.

A Preliminary Self-Help Guide
To Being a Sprig More Parsley

- Be ready to defend the assertion that the glasses in the Holiday Inn are really sanitized for your protection.

- Avoid any man or woman wearing black leather and more than one diagonal zipper.

- Remember these maxims: gravy goes with everything and a good cup of hot tea and the telephone is better than a year of psychotherapy.

- For potluck dinners, volunteer to bring the main dish, a noodle casserole, hot.

- when choosing gifts, aim for things as cute as koala bears, E.T. mittens, potpourri pillows, and Canada mints.

- Trust anyone whose first name ends in *ie, y,* or *i.* Distrust anyone whose name is Lothar.

- When acquaintances start discussing movies with subtitles, pretend you've seen them but say you don't think they make good wholesome films anymore.

The Problem with Parsleys

A sprig of Parsley is an absolute necessity on the Great Roast Beef of Life. But a bunch of Parsley people will really throw any of the other Seasonings into insulin shock. Take that cheerful, non-bickering family you saw at Howard Johnsons last week, joyfully reading "Table Talk" to each other, and dressed in matching look-a-like denim outfits with sweet red-checked bandannas.

Actually, they don't always have to come in bunches to overwhelm the other Seasonings. T.V. preachers, for instance, all are Parsleys.

Then there's your local Tupperware or Amway distributor who sell soap suds and plastic with religious fervor.

Look around you, there's bound to be at least one Parsley in your immediate environs. She's the stick-in-the-mud who insists on including someone who is really too difficult to accommodate in your once-a-month out-of-the-office luncheon. She's the one who doesn't (or won't) understand the punchline of your joke or, worse, will be offended if it's a shade off-color. He's the Cub Scout leader whose idea of a fun weekend is camping with twenty screaming eight-year-olds in the wilderness.

A dinner with the Parsleys is bound to be congealed salad with miniature marshmallows and Turkey á la King on toasted Wonder Bread. You'll recognize their house right away by its overabundance

Parsley pictures looks best in sweet frames.

Images of sugared nature are the Parsley hallmark.

Even Bunny is happy here.

of Americana, real or imagined. Who else would have a spinning wheel in the living room, roosters on the kitchen wallpaper, and pink floral hooked rugs?

It was a Parsley who covered the first extra roll of toilet paper with a crocheted poodle and started people saying, "Have a nice day." A Parsley invented happy faces and plastered them everywhere. Follow the scent of Lysol straight to the Parsleys.

And, when they go on vacation, expect to receive a barrage of picture postcards with messages like, "Williamsburg is so quaint," with hearts dotting every *i*. Go on vacation with Parsleys (if you like bus tours). You'll find them sweetly stubborn and constantly constipated. They'll be ready to head "for the barn" after the first day.

The Parsley Hall of Fame

Women	Men
June Allyson	Frankie Avalon
Francis Bavier	Ken Berry
Barbara Billingsly	Dan Blocker
Billie Burke	Pat Boone
Spring Byington	Charlie Brown
Doris Day	Bill Cullen
Rosemary DeCamp	Roy Clark
Sandra Dee	Perry Como
Mia Farrow	Dennis Day
Annette Funicello	Hugh Downs
Melissa Gilbert	Andy Devine
Florence Henderson	Troy Donahue
June Lockhart	John Daly
Mary Martin	Mike Douglas
Butterfly McQueen	George Gobel
Marilyn Monroe	Monty Hall
Harriet Nelson	David Hartman
Betsy Palmer	Rock Hudson
Jane Pauley	Art Linkletter
Debbie Reynolds	Bert Parks
Marie Osmond	Jim Nabors

Parsley Bunches

Parsleys are the only ones who come in bunches.

The King Family	Lawrence Welk Show cast
The Mormon Tabernacle Choir	The Brady Bunch
The Mouseketeers	The Partridge Family
The Lennon Sisters	Miss Americas
The June Taylor Dancers	Actors in Wrigley Gum
Readers Digest readers	commercials

The Parsley Quiz

Do you think you are a Parsley? Are you one of those tender, open souls who has the milk of human kindness in his heart? Take this little quiz to see if you're made of the right stuff. Answers appear at the end of the quiz.

1. You are planning a party. It's a...

   A. welcome-home party for your British diplomatic friends just back from the Falklands. You've invited all your Latin neighbors and encouraged everyone to discuss the war.

   B. a minimalist party where everyone gathers in your loft, dressed as stripes and dots for an evening of silence.

   C. a birthday party for your honey, at home, with a pink-and-white striped cake and vanilla ice cream. There's just one discreet candle on top of the cake because you don't want your darling to feel old.

2. You open the door of the guest room to awaken your house-guests for a nice, big breakfast. You find yourself witnessing a moment of frenzied romance. You...

   A. run and tell your spouse all about it, describing every sensuous action and enjoying every moment of it.

   B. say, "Mind if I join you?" and jump right in.

   C. turn red, feel your chest break out in a rash, and repeat to yourself, "I didn't see anything, I didn't see anything...."

3. You are given the most godawful decorative ornament ever conceived as a gift from your second grade Brownie buddy. You...

   A. thank her, and give it to someone else as a joke.

   B. thank her, ask her where she got it because you want to give Emma one just like it, then return it for credit.

   C. thank her, keep it on your mantel, and actually learn to love it because she gave it to you.

   The Parsley answer in each case is C.

What's Parsley and What Isn't

Parsley	Not Parsley
Dwight and Mamie Eisenhower.......	Juan and Eva Peron
Family style........................	a la carte
Kleenex boutique facial tissue........	toilet paper
picnics	alfresco dining
Disneyland	42nd Street
a good cheddar...................	sushi
pink	punk
electric organs...................	electric guitars
Barry Manilow...................	Frank Zappa
The Poconoes....................	The Pyrenees
Christmas	Lenin's birthday
Oklahoma!	O Calcutta!
French Impressionists..............	German Expressionists
jockey shorts....................	no shorts
Tinkerbell	The Archangel Gabriel
gingham	Hermione Gingold

The Do-It-Yourself Parsley People List:

Now list your own Parsley acquaintances. Call on them. They are invaluable allies on any volunteer project, stalwart but quiet friends in time of need. Be sure to note on this list who...

1. has a station wagon

2. has a full array of garden tools

3. makes good brownies

4. plays Christmas carols on the electric organ

5. has an ice cream freezer

Your Parsley List: Telephone No.

Parsley pleasure

Chapter Four

Style and Sparkle
PEPPER

Pepper People

PPPPPPPPPPPPPPP OOOOOOOOOOO WWWWWWWWW!

Peppers are HOT. From the stately green bell to the fiery red chili, they **make** fireworks happen for the rest of humanity.

Even as insignificant little berries and seeds ripening in the summer sun, Peppers know they are destined for BIG things. Not content to sit primly on top of your hamburger, they have designs on everyone's entire gastrointestinal system.

But Peppers need time to ripen into that final sharp, biting flavor that makes them famous. Life isn't always easy for them. As little corns, they are too fiery and passionate. They often burn the people they most want to cultivate. Peppers pass in and out of fashion very quickly. One year the green corns are on top, next year the pink. They can't afford to rest on their lettuce.

Applause is the sound Peppers like best. No solitary soliloquies for them. Their talents *deserve* an audience, and they are willing to work for their spotlight. They *know* what it is to try hard and win. They make scintillating conversation and dashing manners into an art form, and, at their very ripest, Peppers are the performers who make you stand up and shout, "Bravo!" with true feeling and appreciation.

Special preparation is the hallmark of Peppers. They are the only spice that is "presented" to diners in a fine restaurant. The Pepper woman plans her presentation. An hour of painful, tortuous calisthenics is followed every night by a luxurious soak in the tub, emersed in expensive bath oils. Never a callous on her foot or an errant hair anywhere, she is groomed perfection...always costumed in the latest and sometimes most outrageous. Her entire being shouts what is new and "coming."

Energy oozes from every one of *his* pores. His magnificent body enjoys the torture of staying that way. He's the smiling marathon runner whizzing past you at the twenty-fourth mile, and when he does put his clothes on, he wears *only* the best.

Peppers are not monogamous beings. They have brief, volcanic love affairs, then move on. They're just too restless to stay in your life forever. And, it's just as well, because their energy saps the strength of normal lovers. The mere mortal can stand only a dash.

Peppers plot their parties, too. After all, parties are the showcases of a Pepper's place in the world. Guests are meticulously chosen so that their party has a chance for an appearance in *Vogue* or *The Maple Valley Sun*. And, don't plan to sneak quietly home from a Pepper party at 11 p.m. Peppers are always ready for one more dance and the champagne never runs out.

In fact, Peppers are rarely still. They live to create a torrent of emotion to sweep the rest of the world away. They stroll only when visiting rich, old relatives at nursing homes. Otherwise, they walk fast, dart, skip, and tap dance through life.

The rest of the Seasonings will just have to admit...Peppers are the sparkle in salads, the bite in pizza, the zip in our lives. We may not love them, but we pay attention to them. They are too hot for most...too fiery...too fiesty...volcanic...complex. We'd love to mix with them, but we know that a pinch is all we are likely to get.

Peppers *may* never get to the White House, nor call someone in New Guinea, but they like to look as if they do — regularly.

The Pepper Quiz

Do you think you are a Pepper? Are you really that dazzler of a soul that sizzles while the rest of humanity sleeps? Take this little quiz to see if you're made of the ripe stuff. Answers appear at the end of the quiz.

1. On an out-island in the Caribbean, you are awakened from a nap at pool-side by disco music. You...

    A. find the fuse box and turn off the power

    B. move to a deserted section of the beach

    C. get up and join the dancing. The day had been quiet, and, after all, if you had not been looking for a little adventure and fun, you would have gone somewhere like Palm Beach or Boca Raton.

2. Aunt Mabel arrives unexpectedly. She presents you with a bottle of Möet and an entire box of Fauchon items. You...

    A. ask her, "What's Möet? What's Fauchon?"

    B. kiss her, sit her on the sofa, get out the family album and call out for pizza

    C. get out the stemware, call your dog (a Lhasa Apso named Baccarat) and the three of you make dinner on the contents of her package

3. You go to sit in your seat at the theater and find another couple also has legitimate tickets for the same seats at the same performance. You...

    A. look through check stubs to see who purchased their tickets first

    B. figure they are probably entitled to the seats, put on your coat, go to the box office to get your money back, and go home

    C. discover that both your weddings were covered in the same society page, decide to share the seats, and end up being invited to their summer place

    The answer in each case is C.

A Preliminary Self-Help Guide To Being a Pinch More Pepper

- In your last will and testament, request that your ashes be scattered from the top floor of Tiffanys.

- Even if you accomplish nothing else, claim you are a graduate of the Erno Laszlo Institute.

- have at least one best-woman-friend named Bianca, Estee, Clarissa, Angelica, Zandra, Gloria, Cha Cha, or Skye.

- Give your children family names but do not, under any circumstances ever call them by their given names. Rather, use "pet" names based on (1) an expensive sport, e.g., "Flyer"; (2) something foreign and preferably French; (3) something at least semi-precious, e.g., Jade, Lapis, and so forth.

- Remember that Lauren Bacall says, "I don't mind the blues in the night as long as they are sapphires."

- Use these words or phrases daily: *ultimate, incomparable, posh, simply staggering, exclusive,* and *amazed.*

The Sins of Peppers

In their desire to be a "glorious yacht, going full-throttle through the great sea of life," Peppers set up such a wake they capsize all small craft in the vicinity.

Peppers, while beautiful and exciting, are not kind. They never stay with little, salt-of-the-earth people for long. They may like them for awhile, enjoy their adoration, but, once they've picked up what there is to learn—the most clever stories, the most interesting friends, the best recipes—they move one.

Being involved with Peppers is like living in a pressure cooker. Most people, unaccustomed to the intensity, are "overdone" in a fraction of their normal time.

Peppers can be dangerous despots. If thwarted, they are selfish tyrants who sulk and order everyone around.

If a Pepper loses his or her beautiful veneer in your presence, BEWARE. The fact that someone knows the truth can be horrifying and unbearable to them. Their unscrupulous selves might become public. Be prepared to run for cover.

Peppers have a cruel sense of humor. They are funny, but you should know that when you laugh, it will be at your, or someone else's expense. Their jokes are ruthlessly pointed and calculating.

Peppers control and dominate all attempts at civilized, group conversation. They turn any topic to *their* subject and proceed to areas where no one else can compete. This is not to imply that their conversation is not interesting...it is! Who else can keep up with stories about spending the summer with Charlie and Di on Malta?

You can waste a lot of postage on Peppers. If you're still sending Christmas cards to someone from whom *you* haven't received one in two years, odds are, it is a Pepper. The other Seasonings envy and "love" the Peppers in their lives. But that affection is not always reciprocated. Parsleys, Garlics, and Gingers are not all that interesting to Peppers in the long run.

The Pepper Hall of Fame	
Women	**Men**
Lauren Bacall	Fred Astaire
Pearl Bailey	Phineas T. Barnum
Shirley Boothe	James Coco
Carol Burnett	Noel Coward
Sarah Bernhardt	Jimmy Durante
Carol Channing	Cary Grant
Cher	Harry Houdini
Phyllis Diller	Spike Jones
Zsa Zsa Gabor	Gene Kelly
Mitzi Gaynor	Jerry Lewis
Judy Garland	Steve Martin
Hedda Hopper	Groucho Marx
Lena Horne	Zero Mostel
Madeline Kahn	Don Rickles
Angela Lansbury	Mickey Rooney
Gypsy Rose Lee	Phil Silvers
Carmen Miranda	Red Skelton
Shirley MacLaine	Tommy Tune
Ethel Merman	Dick Van Dyke
Liza Minelli	Flip Wilson
Louella Parsons	
Zazu Pitts	
Joan Rivers	
Diana Ross	
Gwen Verdon	

What's Pepper and What Isn't

Pepper	Not Pepper
Fred Astaire and Ginger Rogers	Jed Clampett and Minnie Pearl
The Greek Islands	Staten Island
flower arranging	weeding
tap dancing	Polish circle dancing
sable coats	Naugahide ponchos
Rome, Italy	Rome, Georgia
Neiman Marcus	Sears Roebuck
Swan Lake	Lake Okeechobee
folk art	church bazaar crafts
French champagne	French onion dip
designer black silk	Singer Stretch'n'Sew
Beaujolais Nouveaux	Grape soda
The Cleveland Orchestra	Cleveland
Marie Antoinette's cottage in the Garden at Versailles	a pre-assembled garden shed from K Mart
Harry Winston	Kay Jewelers Keepsake Corner
a recipe from *Vogue*	a recipe from *Woman's Day*
hot crab in a chafing dish	Chung King frozen egg rolls on a cookie sheet

The Do-It-Yourself Pepper People List

Now, list your own Pepper acquaintances (if you have any). If you don't, make a list of those you wish you knew. A Pepper is not likely to lend you any of her possessions, but you will want to make a note of which seasonal party is the best given by each of your Pepper acquaintances and who has the nicest tennis courts or the biggest boat. You may not be invited to participate in any of their events, but you can try . . .

Your Pepper List:

Telephone No.

(note second lines, answering services and mobile/marine ship-to-shore lines for yachts. Note TELEX, and Cable Addresses)

_____   _____

_____   _____

_____   _____

_____   _____

_____   _____

Chapter Five

Life and Vitality
GARLIC

Garlic People

Garlics *reek* of life. Put just one of these little white bulbs in your Main Dish. . .and watch out. Ripe, flamboyant, fertile, Garlics will break dance their way through every Saturday night.

Not a quickly passing pleasure, your Garlic friends stay with you. They are loud and energetic, the life of the party, always full of fantastic ideas and projects. You can always count on them to drag the heavy volleyball net to the beach, plan who brings what to the office picnic, and come up with the most powerfull chili. Put them around a camp fire, toasting marshmallows with good buddies, and they'll sing their hearts out. Garlics just love to bubble and simmer in the Great Stew of Life.

Garlics love pigs and people. They delight in every object that is
"fun" and "full-of-life."

Here comes Super Seasoning! For centuries, Garlics have chased away vampires and cleaned out digestive tracts. *He* is Tarzan, Santa Claus, Robin Hood. *She* is Charlie's Angel, Wonder Woman, Tugboat Annie.

Look for all the bumper stickers on their cars. They always have a *Cause*. And when one fails, they'll find another, and another, and another. They never give up hope.

What Garlics lack in subtlety, they make up for in flavor. He is rumpled in a business suit, terrific in jeans, boots and plaid. She is the original "Girl who can't Say No," just too curvaceous for the tailored look. But put her into a swirling swishing skirt, and she'll make your senses reel.

Garlics are always busy...living and loving. No dainty scent, no demure manners, no mystery. Garlics *are* Sex.

But, inside each and every potent bulb, lies the soul of a lily. They are the most generous of Seasonings, capable of great kindness. He is the one who makes sure you have somewhere to go for Thanksgiving. She is the one who makes you a birthday cake after your divorce. Indulgent and indulging, Garlics can forgive you anything but indifference.

The Garlic Quiz

Do you think you are a Garlic? Are you that earthy, lively soul that is the salt of the stew? Take this little quiz to see if you really qualify. Answers appear at the end of the quiz.

1. On your way to your apartment, you pass a neighbor's door. He wants you to come in and join them for a drink at a lively party.

   A. You say, "No. I'm tired, thanks." You go home, stuff cotton in your ears, and hope the beach music they're playing won't keep you awake.

   B. You see the party is a sea of women in caftans and men with plastic pocket protectors and instantly remember you have a splitting headache.

   C. You say, "Great," run over to your place, get some eats, and a rhumba record, and race back.

2. You are designing your dream house. You have a wish list, but number one on your "really need" list is...

   A. built-in display cases for your collection of ceremonial Congolese Tribal headdresses.

   B. a spotlit black tile foyer with a crystal chandelier to greet your guests.

   C. a centralized kitchen where the wall phone has a cord long enough to do dishes, wipe bottoms, answer the front door, fix a meal, and reach the refrigerator full of Miller without interrupting your conversation.

3. You are suddenly awake at 5 a.m. on a Saturday, hours before you need to get up. You...

   A. get up, balance your checkbook, scrub the bathroom tile with scouring powder, and polish every shoe in the house.

   B. get up, count your flat silver, cook and bone fourteen whole chickens to freeze for future use, and refresh your memory on the French names of all the meats and vegetables

   C. think about breakfast, contemplate sex, smile, roll over, and go back to sleep.

The answer in each case is C.

A Preliminary Self-Help Guide
To Being a Squeeze More Garlic

• Have as hobbies only those activities that require exercising at least two parts of the body below the waist.

• Avoid the company of anyone who enjoys quiet reading.

• Have on hand at all times: beer, popcorn, peanut butter, candles, and contraceptives.

• Know that it is one's right to eat Mexican food, Boston baked beans, apples, and cabbage, no matter what the consequences.

• Never own a single bed.

• Learn to play at least two instruments, including your own.

• Never clean out a drawer or throw away anything.

- Firmly believe that there can never be enough working flashlights, wine, pockets, scissors, crayons, big red handkerchiefs, friends who kiss and hug, scotch tape, or Saturdays.

The Problem with Garlics

Garlics thrive in squalor. The word *clutter* has no meaning in their language. In fact, unless you have a medical degree, you should never explore the back shelves of their refrigerators.

They are loud...you hear them coming...and you sometimes wish they'd go away. They take too much of your time, hogging your bedroom and your bathroom, mutilating your toothpaste, and using the last shred of your toilet paper.

Garlics wouldn't think of following directions. They buy unassembled bicycles for their children and put the seat on backwards. Filters of all types—in automobiles and furnaces—are on a decade rotation schedule. Garlics are the only spice who find no embarrassment in having the plumber in to unplug the toilet.

The remains of Garlic good times. Garlics always have the makings of a party on hand for 200 or two.

Garlics rarely finish a project. They are slow and stubborn and hard to move. They think orders are "too limiting." For instance, they are the cooks who figure that if one of something is called for, why not add sixteen? As guests, they are never on time, and when they do arrive they bring nine extra guests and leave late.

If anyone is going to be fat, it's a Garlic. Ah! The jelly-like wobble of a row of Garlics doing the bunny hop.

And, one would think all Garlics had recently returned from a sale of Hawaiian shirts at a discount house. Not only are their color schemes impossible, but they always have a spot in the middle of their tie or a run up the back of their stocking.

- The person who can't give up smoking is a Garlic.

- The person who always overeats is a Garlic.

- The person who forgets to turn off lights and typewriters, who leaves kernels on corn cobs, is a Garlic.

- The person who uses six thicknesses of toilet paper is a Garlic.

- The person who leaves the cork off the wine bottle, the top off the rubber cement or your nail polish is a Garlic.

What's Garlic and What Isn't

Garlic	Not Garlic
Sports trivia	Freudian innuendos
Baked beans	L.L. Bean
Square dancing and polkas	Ballet and Prokofiev
Zane Grey and Louis L'Amour	Jane Austen and Barbara Pym
Timex	Being on time
Needlepoint	Acupuncture
Canadian goose down coats	French goose liver on toast
Beer	Perrier with lime
Touch football	Stamp collecting
Home cooking	Cuisine minceur
Irish setters	Poodles
Hide-a-beds	Chaise lounges
The Thornbirds and *Valley of the Dolls*	*The Iliad* and *The Odyssey*
Boraxo	Nutragena
Plastic party glasses	Tulip stemware
Mr. Goodwrench	Mr. Roger's Neighborhood
Chevy trucks	Chevy Chase, Md.
John Deere	Mommie Dearest
Bourbon and water	Kir

The Garlic Hall of Fame

Women	Men
Ann-Margret	Dan Akroyd
Valerie Bertinelli	Alan Bates
Karen Black	Warren Beatty
Dyan Cannon	Harry Belafonte
Maria Callas	Jean-Paul Belmondo
Bo Derek	Dirk Bogart
Joyce DeWitt	Marlon Brando
Loretta Lynn	Tom Selleck
Jane Russell	Omar Sherif
Dolly Parton	Sylvester Stallone
Beverly Sills	Danny Thomas
Sissy Spacek	John Travolta
Donna Summer	Rip Torn
Mary Travers	Rudolf Valentino
Tina Turner	John Wayne
Vivian Vance	
Raquel Welch	
Shelly Winters	

The Do-It-Yourself Garlic People List

Now, list every Garlic you know. This will make a great party list. Be sure to note on this list who...

1. will keep your children, pets, or out-of-town relatives overnight

2. has Fritos, French Onion Dip, potato chips, ketchup, popcorn, Oreos, Bacos, pretzels, beer or twist-top wine always ready for action

3. keeps K-Y Jelly and will let you borrow half a tube for tonight

4. has a never-ending supply of juicy (explicit) books you can borrow

5. knows how to get the hair out of the bathtub drain

Your Garlic List: Telephone No.

_____   _____

_____   _____

_____   _____

_____   _____

Chapter Six

Intellect and Wit
GINGER

Ginger People

Its form seems simple, as does any root's, but Ginger has character.
You may not even notice its flavor at first bite. Actually, it doesn't
want you to. But your appreciation of Ginger grows with your own
sophistication.

As Ginger matures, it creates its own "look"—irregular, gnarled,
absolutely unique. As you study it at the store, you'll notice that
each root has its own distinct personality and shape that reflect its
past, its own efforts to grow, and its own imagination.

So it is with Ginger people. They consider themselves mellow
gold. People will say of *her*, "Oh she is so smart and attractive."
They do not say she is "foxy," "sexy," "dazzling," and certainly
not an "easy lay." She is handsome, elegant, and always correct.
Ginger women wear costly but simple jewelry, cleverly tied scarves,
solid colors, or small geometric prints.

He is not Gingerbread Man...no sweet, happy face and open
arms. His expression to strangers is cool, aloof, and neutral. His
upper lip is perpetually stiff in public. He wears undershirts under
every kind of clothing because they keep him cool in summer and
warm in winter. He wears good shoes because they have to last.
Over-the-calf socks are Ginger socks...no unsightly hairy leg peek-
ing out under his suit.

Like all good roots, Gingers make their private home out of sight.
They burrow deep into the soil. There, they refine themselves,
establishing their character and preparing themselves for the world.
Then, supremely self-confident, they quietly emerge. People often
think that all babies are little Parsleys. Not Gingers. They are born
as little "Belgian carrots" or itsy-bitsy parsnips. They are thumb-
suckers and observers, interested in the world around them but
not grabbing at it. They may talk late, but they always talk in full
sentences.

Ginger's flavor is sharp, bitter, sour, and sweet...all at once. Gingers are complex. They do aspire to greatness, but it's intellectual or artistic greatness. Their ultimate goal is to be better than everyone else. Hence, they are rarely completely satisfied. You can tell a Ginger is satisfied when he doesn't criticize.

And because they've spent so much time underground, contemplating their universe, Gingers have IDEAS and OPINIONS. They are critical and demanding, preoccupied with detail and perfection. They like old culture, old paintings, old furniture... these are things to be trusted.

Artful Gingers surround themselves with only "quality" items for pancakes or mantle. References are always to intellect and discernment.

In the romance department, Gingers are late bloomers. But when they do bloom, it is into a rich flower. Their initial problem is that they have to think about everything and intellectualize it almost beyond recognition. "How far do I go on the third date? Am I making too much of a commitment too soon? If this is a mistake, how much will I regret it, and for how long?" These are desperate questions for a maturing Ginger. But once they have defined their "love," their thoughtfulness, attention, and desire to fulfill your needs are unrivaled among the Seasonings.

The Ginger Quiz

Do you think you are a Ginger? Are you that discerning and perceptive soul who survives through razor-sharp intellect? Take this little quiz to see if you're up to crystalizing. Answers appear at the end of the quiz.

1. You win first choice at the gift table as winner of the door prizes. You pick...

    A. "Doris Day's Greatest Hits" and "The Pat Boone Christmas Album"

    B. four cases of generic beer

    C. season passes to the museum lecture series

2. Your charity donation for the year was...

    A. fifty dollars in cash to the Jerry Lewis Telethon

    B. fifty hours of volunteer service in the "ghetto" helping applicants fill out the paperwork for public assistance

    C. fifty dollar check to the symphony ball where you will be listed as a patron

3. You are walking down the street and people begin to turn around and look at you. You...

    A. love it, but pretend not to take notice. They are admiring your children, each in an outfit that is brand new, expensive, and ultimately fashionable

    B. love it. They are admiring you in a clingy new leather jumpsuit under which you aren't wearing a stitch

    C. hate it. This would not occur, normally; and if it did, it would have to be a mistake

The answer in each case is C.

A Ginger woman's classic kilt, pleated and prim, and correct for every daytime occasion. The style is the same she's worn since school days.

A Preliminary Self-Help Guide
To Being a Sliver More Ginger

- Always have on hand at least one of the following groups in its entirety...

  A. four types of mustard, two of which must be imported;

  B. three types of crackers, none of which can be Ritz, saltines, or Triscuits;

  C. seven bottles of wine, none with twist tops.

- Play tennis, bike ride, or swim. Do not twirl a baton or perform aerobic dances in public, and never have as a hobby any craft that involves gimp, dried beans, or egg cartons.

- Never go for a drink with anyone you can't imagine having the season symphony subscription.

- Always try to edit your conversation *before* it is spoken.

- Name your pets after any individual who is unlikely to come up before the 300-level literature courses. Do *not* name your pet after fun food ("Cupcake," "Cookie," or "Muffin,") things to drink ("Brandy," "Whiskey," or "Cocoa") or energetic descriptive adjectives ("Perky," "Thumper," or "Spinner"). You might consider not having a pet at all.

- Remember, Oscar Wilde said, "I have simple tastes. I am always satisfied with the Best."

The Horrors of Being a Ginger

Gingers can be unbearable. They disagree with everything. Snide, backbiting, and acid, they can be so bitter in concentrated doses that they can spoil everything for forty feet around them. The Ginger woman's not called "Lady with a Spear" without reason. The same wit that comes up with zinging, funny comments can cut you in such a subtle way, that you may never recover.

Gingers' opinions are so strong that their finding an agreeable midcourse is as rare as a feminine hygiene ad on "Walt Disney."

A Ginger's coffee or pencil mug

Gingers can be brusk. They'll end a coversation EXACTLY when they deem it necessary. The telephone answering machine was invented by a Ginger who was always at home, but had no intention of talking to just *anyone*.

Gingers also invented Dutch Treat dinners, single-serve packages, and those paper cups with FULL marked one inch below the top. It was a Ginger who installed "Bus your own table" signs at fast-food restaurants. And, they're the ones who first thought to put cheap liquor in a bottle with the expensive label on it.

If you were looking forward to your neighborhood block party, your Ginger partner could ruin it for you by grumbling and complaining all the way there.

Gingers can be excellent cooks, but they cook for adventure, not day-to-day eating. Gingers set the table and get out the best for themselves. In fact, Gingers delight in being alone.

You may find yourself feeling like a placemat if you attempt to break in on their thoughts. Soliloquies were invented by Gingers; so was talking to oneself. They are their own best audience.

The Ginger Hall of Fame

Women	Men
Joan Baez	Woody Allen
Anne Bancroft	Yul Brenner
Candace Bergen	Humphrey Bogart
Anita Bryant	Walter Brennan
Joan Crawford	Truman Capote
Colleen Dewhurst	Robert DeNiro
Sally Fields	David Frost
Valerie Harper	W. C. Fields
Jean Harlow	Art Garfunkel
Audrey Hepburn	Richard Gere
Katherine Hepburn	Richard Harris
Glenda Jackson	Hugh Hefner
Dianne Keaton	Dustin Hoffman
Vivian Leigh	Laurence Olivier
Ali Macgraw	Vincent Price
Natalia Makarova	Tony Randall
Joni Mitchell	Rex Reed
Mary Tyler Moore	George Segal
Kim Novak	Bobby Short
Carly Simon	Paul Simon
Maggie Smith	Frank Sinatra
Maureen Stapleton	David Susskind
Meryl Streep	Andy Warhol
Barbra Streisand	
Joanne Woodward	

What's Ginger and What Isn't

Ginger	Not Ginger
oil paintings	paintings on velvet
fresh linen	freshly soiled diapers
white Bordeaux	Ripple Ruby Chablis
psychotherapy	encounter groups
museum docent	McDonalds counter attendant
Gourmet magazine on coffee table	*National Enquirer* in the john
taupe slacks	wet t-shirts
crisp vegetables	canned peas
Alistaire Cook and Jackie Onassis	Buddy Hackett and Joan Rivers
the results of the Judgment of Paris	the results of the Clay-Liston fight
a Siamese named Pocahontas	a parakeet named Perky
boxer shorts	fishnet bikini briefs
a gold stick pin	British penny earrings
Pears poached in wine	Cool whip on jello

The Do-It-Yourself Ginger List

Now, list all your Ginger acquaintances. Ask their opinion only if you really want to hear it. They can be quite acidic in their criticism, but no other Seasoning will have thought the problem over so completely.

Gingers have great things to borrow, but you will have to prove yourself before you'll have free access to any of them. If you are up to their standards, they will be able to tell you right off if they have the item you want and in which side of what drawer it is kept. If they cook, they have an unlimited supply of superb recipes others would consider gourmet. They can usually remember birthdays and are excellent sources for solving matters of diplomacy or etiquette. A Ginger on your side is an invaluable ally.

Your Ginger List: **Telephone No.**

Chapter Seven

Put Yourself in Mint Condition

Herbopsychiatric theory includes a philosophy of prudent investing strategy for every one of every Seasoning...

Put your money where your roots are. Thus, if your money is correctly managed, according to the savor of your Seasoning, the return it reaps will be enormous in growth and satisfaction.

The Parsley Method

Parsley money is best kept in a few large bunches, rather than garnished too thinly. Passbook savings accounts, IRA's and Keoghs are perfect Parsley nest eggs.

Do not overlook the advantages of money market funds or certificates of deposit, either. Just as the Parsley plant thrives in ordinary soil, Parsley money thrives in what other Seasonings consider mundane places. You know better. You'll be safe and they'll be sorry.

The Garlic Point-of-View

Spend your money and enjoy. If you invest in anything, make it people and experiences.

Garlics should follow the words of that great American Garlic philosopher, Dolly Gallagher Levi, who often quoted the words of her dear, departed husband, Ephraim: "Money is like manure. You have to spread it around and encourage things to grow, for it to be any good."

The Pepper Procedure

Go for it.

Invest wherever your intuition takes you!

Gold mines in Libya, diamonds in Alaska, silver in Indiana, emeralds in Colombia, platinum in New Jersey.

If you'd like to wear it, loads of others would, too.

And, don't forget to invest in yourself. Many a Pepper would rather wear the bankroll, than endure the boredom of financial security.

The Ginger Programme

The Ginger investor investigates and ponders carefully before any action, whatsoever, is taken. But after this lengthy contemplation, Ginger money is always placed in prudent, stable stocks. Blue Chips are, perhaps, the most satisfying to our careful Ginger.

But you might also try putting your money into collectibles, like art and antiques. Here your attention to detail and research can pay off handsomely.

Chapter Eight

Spiceology 202

Your Herbal Palette: The Spicey Families You Belong To...

Now that you know your Seasoning—or at least your dominant flavor—you should know a little about your relatives. You and your Seasoning have some in-laws. And, like all relatives, some you will be glad to have, and others you'll only acknowledge out of kindness to your mother.

Every Seasoning is a part of a larger family of similar herbs or spices. No two of us are exactly the same degree of Parsley, Garlic, or whatever. This is why, even though you and your Aunt Bertha are both the same Seasoning, you never agree on anything of consequence.

Here comes the complicated part:

How can a Jet-Set Movie Star in Monte Carlo and a third-grade school teacher from Shackle Island, Tennessee, *BOTH BE PEPPERS?* Well, easy. Each in his own environment is a Pepper. Both are Peppers, but they are not necessarily the same *type* of Pepper. They are Peppers in their individual soups. Consider the following...

• Leon Trotsky was a Pepper. He was a Red Pepper.

• Ben Vereen and Diana Ross are absolutely Black Peppers.

• Woody Woodpecker is probably Paprika.

• Scarlet O'Hara is a Bell(e) Pepper.

Perhaps you don't like your Seasoning. For instance, you may not want to be a Parsley. Consider this: all leaves are in the Parsley family. You may find *you* are a BASIL, for instance. There's nothing *tansy* about that!

Study the lists of the members of each family. You can apply them in two VERY direct ways to your life.

1. *You will realize more than ever the variety in the nature of people.* You know a woman who is a Ginger, but she isn't clever enough to be as snide as Gingers usually are. Check out the list. You may discover that she is really a Rutabaga.

2. *You can delight in the harmonious unions of mixing the related herbs and spices in your cooking.* Now that you know what goes with what in nature, you will be able to predict what will go with what in your stomach! And you will know *exactly* what to feed your friends and family next time they come over for a visit.

PARSLEY

The Leaf Family

Parsley	Marjoram	Dillweed	Seaweed
Bay leaf	Thyme	Bee Balm	Crabgrass
Sage	Peppermint	Chamomile	Marijuana
Oregano	Spearmint	Tansy	Coriander
Basil	Lemon balm	Watercress	Angelica
	Lemon verbena	Woodruff	

PEPPER

The Fruit Family (Includes Nuts, Flowers, and Shells)

Black pepper	Paprika	Cloves	Dill seeds
White pepper	Jalapeno pepper	Mustard	Ginko
Cayenne	Tabasco	Mace	Osage oranges
Green bell peppers	Nutmeg	Anise	Golden pepper
Red bell peppers	Cinnamon	Poppy	

GINGER

The Root Family

Ginger	Baby Belgian carrots	Parsnips	Turnips
Sassafras	Radishes	Rutabagas	Horseradish

GARLIC

The Bulb Family

Garlic cloves and buds	Shallots	Leeks	Spanish onions
Garlic heads	Spring onions	Bermuda onions	Big white onions
Chives	Pearl onions	Vidalia onions	Ramps

Chapter Nine

Color Me Parsley

A Complete Color Guide Based on Your Seasoning

It is a proven fact that there are certain shades of colors that will make you look healthy, feel happy, and radiate a glorious sense of well-being.

Wearing your colors will be like fertilizing yourself: you'll blossom like never before.

Ignore what others have told you about your skin tone, hair color, and eye color. All that matters is that your palette of colors suits the tasty palette of your Seasoning.

Remember: Be Alive With Color

Never build your wardrobe or decorate your bedroom with color principally from another palette. Take the basics from your own colors or you'll soon look as though you suffer from root rot.

Never wear colors from another palette next to your face or your complexion will look insipid as week-old mushrooms.

Certain colors *EVERYONE* can wear...Earth Brown, Grass Green, Sunshine Yellow, Sky Blue, Cherry Red, Cloud White, Midnight Black, or Sunset Gold. When in doubt, try one of those.

WRONG COLOR   **R**IGHT COLOR

Hp.D. Kathleen Hughes, A PARSLEY, is overpowered by the vicious Ginger houndstooth fabric in peppery Vogue Violet. But look how radiant she looks in the sweet "I love bears" Parsley print of Bluebird Blue and Candy Cane on Wonder Bread White. *(Believe it or not, these are absolutely untouched photos. Kathleen's makeup is identical in both photos.)*

Your Growing Color Palette

PARSLEY	PEPPER
Puritan Pink Candy Cane	Hot, Hot Pink Plaza Pink
Honest Red	Tabasco Red Red Snapper
Communion Wine	Rockefeller Rouge
Welch's Grape Shrinking Violet	Star Sapphire Vogue Violet
Walden Pond Aqua	St. Tropez Aqua
Bluebird Blue	Blazing Blue
Turquoise Twirl	Peacock Terribly Turquoise
Ensign Blue	Fleet Admiral Navy
Apple Green Yodel Green Parsley Green	Limelight Money Green Green Envy Emerald
Ivory Snow Wonder Bread White	Possesive White Platinum White Diamond Dazzle
Tender Taupe Buddy Beige Sweet Honey	Buffo Beige Teuscher Taupe Onassis Oyster Town & Country Caramel
Baby Blankie Yellow Buttercup	YELLow
Georgia Peach Settled Salmon Kind Coral	Mellon Melon Flashy Flesh
Orange Sherbet Orange Pekoe	Armandi Orange
Hershey's Kiss Brown	Hot Chocolate Pulsating Paprika Cinnamon Nutmeg
Dove Grey	Sterling Silver Gray
Basic Black	Black Magic

To Compare Colors, Read Across The Charts

Your Growing Color Palette

GARLIC

Passion Pink
Pecker Pink

Cruising Crimson
Randy Rose

Jug Burgundy

Lascivious Lavender
Plump Plum

Hot-Tub Aqua

Hubba-Bubba Blue

Navajo Turquoise
Scuba Blue

Blue Jeans Blue

Astroturf Green
Untamed Evergreen
Hunter Green

Whoopee White
Garlic Clove White

Bosom Beige
Sun Tan
Peanut Butter

Pina Colada Yellow

Sauna Salmon
Persimmon Pucker

Tequila Sunrise

Chocoholic Brown
Bowel Brown
Beer Stain Brown
Coppertone Bronze

Charcoal Grill Grey

Blackout Black

GINGER

Pre-Columbian Pink
Picky Pink

Reserved Ruby

Haut Brion Bourdeaux

Aubergine
Cassis

Bottled Aqua

Ice Blue

Antique Turquoise

Blue Book Blue

Jaded Green
Chartreuse
Olive Drab

Lovely but Lonesome White
Carrara White

Bittersweet
Ginza Camel
Ginger
Seal Point Oyster

Dijon Mustard

Smoked Scottish Salmon
Evelyn Crabtree Peach

Pumpkin Mousse

Godiva Brown
Antique Walnut
Rubbed Mahogany
Tooled Leather Brown

Griege

Polished Ebony

To Compare Colors, Read Across The Charts

Chapter Ten

An Instant Diet for Every Seasoning

For centuries, humanity has sought the perfect diet, one that slims and revitalizes without the loss of any nutritional values. Herbs and spices have always been considered medicinal and healthy. Whether wild or cultivated, selective introduction has brought pleasure to the palette and improvement to the body.

Now through modern herbopsychiatric advances, you can use your Seasoning's special diet for whatever result you choose. Here are the basic rules you must follow...

1. When you are a little under the weather, let your diet be dominated by food from *your own* Seasoning. You'll feel like your old self almost immediately.

2. When you want to be especially spicy, embellished with flavors other than your own, try a diet dominated by the tastes of *other* Seasonings. For example...

   A. Before a weekend with disagreeable relatives, dine on meals composed of, or strongly seasoned with, members of the Parsley bunch. You'll discover docile and pleasant traits in yourself that your soul has been saving for you.

   B. Focus on root vegetables and Ginger-related Seasonings prior to divorce proceeding or confrontations with Internal Revenue auditors.

   C. Garlic, onions and true bulbs, of any sort, are excellent gastrointestinal preparation for visits to nudist colonies or co-ed communal bathing spas.

   D. Pepper and all its relations are perfect dietary supplements before cheerleading tryouts or other public appearances that scare you to death.

Parsley Food

Because they are the crisp leaves of nature, Parsley food helps you stay fresh, spry and regular. Here's a sample menu for a Parsley day. Stick to this and you'll be a slender stalk in no time.

Breakfast

One coddled egg, in your favorite
    egg cup, with parsley garnish
A glass of lettuce juice
Toast with mint jelly
Herbal tea

Lunch

Green salad with watercress,
    dandelion greens, salad burnet,
    endive and chicory, tossed with
    herb vinegar
A glass of May wine with woodruff

Cocktail Time

Mint julep
Steamed artichoke with sage
    vinaigrette

Dinner

Basil pesto on steamed spinach
Lettuce salad (*including iceberg,
    Boston and red leaf*) with oregano
    dressing
Oriental green tea

Calories: *Not many, but to diet, take
demure, small portions*

Pepper Food

Keep it fiery and keep yourself dashing around. Pepper food can be richer and more caloric than other people's fare because Pepper people burn calories, as they sizzle with energy. Here's a sample menu for a Pepper day. Stick to this and you will move so fast you'll give off smoke.

Petit Dejeuner

A glass of Perrier on the rocks with
    a twist
A croissant with cinnamon/apple
    butter and poppy seed danish

Dejeuner

A glass of champagne
White asparagus with nutmeg
    hollandaise
Green and red bell pepper salad
Cup of coffee, ground from fresh
    beans imported from Kenya

Cocktail Time

Bloody Mary with extra cayenne
Stuffed jalapena peppers or brie
    with hot pepper jelly

Dinner

A last glass of champagne
Nova Scotia salmon with green
    peppercorns
Stuffed peppers
Pears, poached in red wine with
    mace

Calories: *Peppers burn up fat so fast, calories aren't much of a problem. Other Seasonings should beware the high fat content in this diet can turn you into a blimp in a
matter of days.*

Ginger Food

The root family of which Ginger is a member is bland on one end, and bitter on the other. Ginger food is excellent for dieting, however, since it provides the satisfaction of bulk and mastication. Here is a sample menu for a jolly Ginger day. Stick to this diet and you may be able to see in the dark.

Breakfast

Toasted bran muffin with gingered pear preserves
Two glasses of turnip juice
Sassafras tea with no sugar, no milk, no nothing

Cocktail Time

T.S. Elliot Cocktail (*Parsnip juice with vodka*)
Raw turnip sliced with horseradish dip

Luncheon

Shredded carrot salad
Harvard beets
A glass of ginger ale

Dinner

Baked celery root
Jerusalem artichokes in ginger dressing
Carrot cake
Root beer

Calories: *An entire day of Ginger food makes you lose your appetite. This is exactly why it is such an effective diet.*

Garlic Food

Garlic food is easy to prepare and often requires only unwrapping. Here's a sample menu for a Garlic day. Stick to this one, and you'll break the sound barrier. Everything in the Garlic diet is perfectly suited to being a leftover and reheated or eaten cold directly out of the refrigerator.

Breakfast

Fried egg with grilled red onions or 1 heaping helping of yesterday's chili, cold and greasy
Onion bagel
Lite beer with green onion swizzle

Cocktail Time

Gusto & Guts Special (*beer with a pickled onion in it*)
Fried onion rings with ketchup

Lunch

Leek soup
Onion-flavored breadsticks or onion melba toasts
Milkshake (*choice of flavor, or more than one if undecided*)

Supper

French onion soup
Rare steak with garlic puree
Baked onions with chives
Marinated raw onion salad with garlic croutons and bottled creamy scallion dressing
Kahlua & cream and/or pina coladas

Calories: *Don't even bother to keep track of calories on Garlic food days. If you want to lose weight, refer to the Ginger or Parsley diets.*

Chapter Eleven

Herbal Dressings

Now that you know your Seasonal colors, *(See Chapter Nine, page 47)* you are ready to put together that perfect wardrobe that works for you on all occasions.

Pictorial Imagery of The Seasonings
From Baroque & Rococo Sources

Herbopsychiatry has its roots in ancient times. Then, unlike today, there was a fairly common agreement on the way in which the Seasonings could be intelligibly and effectively represented visually. *(On the following pages, you will find modern versions of The Seasonings.)* Here are the ancient & medieval allegorical personifications.

Parsley

Pepper

Ginger

Garlic

T.P.S.
The Total
Parsley Style...
for women

You'd really have to work hard to achieve this *Total Parsley Style.* Rarely has anyone succeeded in incorporating so many Parsley elements on one simple body, but study each suggested Parsley piece and try all of them on. If you are a Parsley, you'll look and feel your very best whenever you wear anything listed below.

1. *Plastic rain hat.* Always kept neatly folded in your purse, unless you get caught in one of those sudden rain showers. The Parsley woman has her hair "done" once a week, and she never wants to lose her "just flipped" look.

2. *Oval barrettes.* Inherited from her childhood (cloisonne or real gold) or recently purchased for a more up-to-date look in pastel plastics.

3. *Bluebird glasses.* It's hard to find these cute little glasses topped with sweet little bluebirds. You may have to settle for pink or blue plastic ones and glue the birds in place on their peaks with Crazy Glue. Sometimes the five-and-dime has Mickey Mouse or Donald Duck hidden behind those rude modern glasses. Look carefully, these are a must.

4. *Circle pin.* We know you'd never throw this classic item away. To emphasize its purity, tuck tiny silk or plastic or even real violets inside it.

5. *Pearls.* Your Parsley pearls can be snap-apart or the real thing, but they are a must morning, noon, or night because they always look perfect with whatever you are wearing, except maybe your flannel Granny nightie.

6. *Garland sweater.* The classic cardigan is your sweater. Dress it up with appliques like this precious teddy bear or your own initials.

7. *Print blouse.* The tinier and cuter the print element, the better. Be sure it has that chaste rounded collar and soft pastel color. Flowers and birds, hearts and rainbows are best TPS patterns.

8. *Soft bow sash.* A romantic element you may tie tidily right in the middle of your stomach. Never push it jauntily to one side, it will ruin your look. (Only in your gingham apron should you wear a bow in the back. It is also pardonable on your square-dancing skirt.)

9. *Hankie.* Always tuck it into your sleeve for quick use. Try lace for evening, kleenex for early morn.

10. *Gloves.* Other spices may have thrown away their proper white gloves, but not you. You know what is correct. Besides they give your outfit that "dressed-up" look you try to achieve.

11. *Full ruffled skirt.* Here's a marvelous look you can make all by yourself. You know that ruffled country curtain you were about to throw away? DON'T. Convert it into the most darling Parsley skirt of all, the country ruffled skirt. You can even keep the balled fringe around the ruffle, if you like. That cute felt bunny is a finishing touch you won't want to miss.

12. *Bermuda bag.* You can change the covers to match every outfit. You may even wish to make yourself a cute little closet "cover" hanger to keep them coordinated neatly with your outfits.

13. *Knitting.* The Parsley woman is never without a craft or project to keep her hands busy. She's knitting herself another Garland sweater or a pair of little booties or argyles for her nephew. Remove your gloves for projects.

14. *Decoy.* We recommend this cunning little duck for that unusual gift. Make it out of macaroni shells or pine cones or whatever you find in your craft basket.

15. *Anklets.* The Parsley woman has always worn anklets, even when they weren't in style. These with lace tops and tiny tailored bows are the height of fashion for everyone. Coordinate the colors to go with your outfit. *(See page 48.)*

16. *Mary Janes.* You never outgrow these, Parsley ladies. Shiny, gleaming, flat and comfy, they are your ultimate dress shoe.

17. *Quilted pillow.* Another craft idea for you "crafty" Parsleys. Put it on your gingham settee, carry it on the bus for your back, give it to an appreciative Parsley friend or relative—its uses and style never grow old.

A tender Parsley tam

T.P.S.
The Total
Parsley Style...
for men

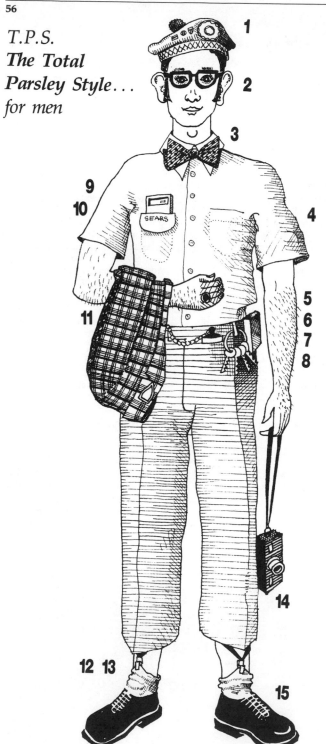

1

2

3

9
10

4

11

5
6
7
8

12 13

14

15

Parsley men, you may not think it possible to achieve this perfect Parsley mien. It will take some hard work, but anyone who can get his yard looking that immaculate should be able to put his Parsley wardrobe into the pristine order prescribed here:

1. *Ethnic hat.* Parsleys are always searching for their roots. Buy that ethnic hat you've been craving, like this jaunty Highland tam, set with a knowing peak on one side. Join the St. Andrews Society, or whatever, and just BE.

2. *The sideburns with neat trim haircut.* Here's another way you can combine your urge to be "with it" and your innate need for tidiness. Let your sideburns GROW...get the rest neatly trimmed. So what if everyone else has short hair now? Join the bushy sideburn set...and feel safe doing so.

3. *Bow tie.* It's sporty, it's neat, it sets off your Adam's apple. It answers your Parsley penchant for flair. Try some of the colors in your special Parsley Palette for unique effects. *(See page 48.)* Other seasonings will trust you in this tie.

4. *Short-sleeved white shirt, summer or winter.* Always worn over your clean white t-shirt, this classic shirt keeps you cool in summer, and no one will know it's there in winter if you keep your sporty jacket on. It goes with everything in your wardrobe and eliminates the need to ponder over shirts in those rushed mornings before work. Even looks good with your Bermudas for yard work.

5. *Pedometer.* Wear it all the time. It's very interesting to keep track of how far you've walked since New Year's. Mark your mileage in your little notebook every evening before bed. It's an accessory you shouldn't be without.

6. *Class ring.* Don't ever lose this piece of fascinating identification.

7. *Keyring on belt.* Held by a clever clasp over your waistband. You'll never be locked out.

8. *Pocket watch.* We hope it's been inherited from your father, but if not, pretend it is. Polish it during business meetings to impress your colleagues.

9,10. *Calculator in plastic pocket protector.* Always handy for quick calculations.

11. *Madras sports coat with Sunday school attendance pin.* This jacket has so many Parsley colors in it, it will go with everything in your wardrobe. Wear a sterling Sunday school pin on your lapel (men's social society pin or Boy Scout pin) and everyone will *know* you're a proud Parsley.

12,13. *Short socks and garters.* Difficult to find but available if you search. These are a must, and, with garters, even though high rise socks are more popular. There's no reason to throw out the short ones that are still perfectly good.

14. *Camera with wrist strap.* You Parsley devil! You always capture that embarrassing posture or "candid" cute shot. Make sure you have your camera ready for a quick snapshot anywhere, any time for *people* pictures.

15. *Classic Army shoes.* Don't you dare throw them away! They're sensible and last forever. Just keep them highly polished.

NOT SEEN: You know about the crisp white t-shirt, but don't forget your 100% cotton or partially polyester white jockey shorts.

A Parsley man can wear this shirt under every outfit.

T.P.P.
The Total
Pepper Pizazz...
for Women

Peppers like show. Everything you put on should shout to the world that you have style and courage...that you're on your way up. Don't leave home without your Pepper polish and you'll feel fiesty all day long. Wow 'em, Pepper ladies!

1. *Matador feather chapeau.* Assertive yet feminine, this hat tops your Pepper look. With its brim set at a jaunty angle, feather fluttering, this hat will bring you the applause you crave. Try a neat, sexy little black veiled hat for those glamorous evenings out.

2. *The geometric gloss hair cut.* The Pepper woman always looks cut from a hairstyle guide. Her hair is sleek and gleaming, gorgeously groomed.

3. *Large, dramatic, flashing earrings.* No matter what the size of your ears, you want them to be glistening with glamour, but discouraging to slobberers. Try geometric shapes in flashing gold (never silver) or a large chandelier of diamonds for essential chic.

4. *Wreaths and wreaths of expensive-looking necklaces.* Great for twirling to emphasize your statements about all and sundry. Consult your Pepper Palette *(page 48)* for the most outrageous color combinations and make sure every bead and bauble bounces as you strut along.

5. *Ever-present sunglasses.* Rain or shine, be sure you have them tucked somewhere on your person...your belt, your hat, your garter. They really make a statement about the drama in you.

6. *Navajo belt.* No Pepper outfit is complete without the largest most dramatic of accessories, particularly the belt. This one emphasizes your tiny waist but can't be unbuckled unless you want it to be; bought when they were cheap and unstylish and yours made the rage.

7. *Boa.* Like the Parsley woman, you don't like to have idle hands, but you use yours to talk. A long, fluffy boa is the apostrophe you need for each scintillating point. Be sure to hit someone in the eye with it. He'll love it.

8. *Noisy bangles.* Jingle your bracelets...Metal clangs, stones click, and Lucite (never call it plastic) waaaps. Select for sound combination, glitter, and luscious color scheme. Let them ride on your arms at all times.

9. *Small beaded bag.* Great for carrying little but mad money. Let HIM carry everything else.

10. *Fish net or patterned stockings.* Don't forget to let your legs make just as dramatic a statement as the rest of your body. They should dance with energy and these stockings will do it for you. A slim seam up the back of your legs completes this priceless look.

11. *High, high heels.* Boots, pumps, sandals...your foot should never be flat. You want to be able to grind your heel in the face of humanity, but no one else can run as fast you can in these stunners. Keep them in suede, satin, or patent leather, and you'll never go wrong.

12. *Puffs, poofs, buckles, and bows.* Never, never, never wear a plain anything. You want to be noticed!

13. *Assertive flowers.* We recommend these bright orange Birds of Paradise for showing everyone you're having a big glamorous "do" this very evening and making them feel left out because they weren't invited.

14. *Crisp, new shopping bag from the most expensive store in town.* If you can't afford to shop there, at least carry their shopping bag. Make sure it's new, so it looks like you just left the premises with some exciting new purchase. You can keep the contents shrouded in tissue to heighten the mystery.

Dazzle, flamboyance and flair exemplify Pepper accessories.

T.P.P.
The Total Pepper Pizazz...
for men

Smooooooooooth and sulkingly silky, that's you, Peppers. Follow these Pepper platitudes and SUCCEED.

1. *Hair plastered down and combed straight back.* Daring, dashing, blown back by the winds of fortune (but held in place by Vitalis).

2. *Mirrored sunglasses.* Reflect your admirers' stares but hide your passionate soul.

3. *Stand-up collar and cuffs.* Nothing lies down when you're around. Even your collar and cuffs stand up and take notice.

4. *Ferocious animal motifs.* Roaring jaguars, snarling lions, pythons, cobras, Jaws I and II. Here, Pepper man wears Oriental embroidered dragon to deepen the mystery and drive he represents.

5. *Heavy-weight I.D. bracelet.* Name engraved on everyone's memory.

6. *Cigarette holder.* Use it with flair, even if you don't smoke. Should be antique or made of fine metals, expensive and daring.

7. *Cravat with stick pin.* Your tie should have a silky shine, but with your style, even a cowboy bandanna worn with the proper aplomb will qualify.

8. *Conspicuous gold jewelry; wedding band or small signet ring forbidden.* Try another identification tag on your gold necklace. Be sure you leave your shirt way open at the neck to show off everything you've got, above the waist that is.

9. *Travel bag with lift tickets and "with-it" vacation spot labels all over it.* Even if you're not going anywhere or have never been, don't let anyone else know. Buy tags at pawn shops. You must look as if you're *always* on your way somewhere special.

10. *Cosmetics.* Not just cologne, this means the Clinique for Men full regime: cleanser, scruffing lotion, moisturizer, wrinkle stick, bronzer. You want to look GOOD.

11. *Pants that show off the things one would only know showed by checking in a three-way mirror.* Painted-on jeans when the canvas is fully primed are best; but stretch jeans can be worn when there is plenty of sirloin to fill them. HINT: Matadors and ballet stars augment with handkerchiefs. So can you.

12. *White, two-tone, or tri-tone shoes.* Flashy-y.

Peppers use even their dresser top as a display area. Note the allusion to exalted ancestry, ferocious nature, and expensive origin. Large crystal obelisks speak for themselves.

T.G.G.
The Total
Garlic Gusto...
for women

Show the world you reek of life, Ms. Garlic, in every part of your beautiful, round body. You may think it impossible to make your every elemental outfit a reeking roar of excitement, but study this sexy miss for all the necessary clothing pieces to complete your working wardrobe.

1. *The sporty visor.* It shades your lustrous eyes from the sun when you're playing hard· and playing hard-to-get (briefly, of course).

2. *Sporty, full, fluffy hair.* Your hair should always look as though you have just climbed out of bed. Wear it as casually and wildly as you can.

3. *Accessories.* Try to do without too many. They'll get in the way of quick undressing or strenuous activities like lolling on the beach or batting a volley ball. One long dangling earring, for instance, says it all, and flashes promise.

4. *Ruffles, swishes, swirls, and lace.* . .A blouse that molds your figure and flutters is what you should wear. Try colors from your special Garlic Palette, the more the merrier. *(See page 49.)*

5. *Tight, tight, emphatic belt.* Cinch that waist in. It makes the rest of your figure plump out nicely.

6. *Name tag.* You want to know everyone, so why not let everyone know you. If you can't have your name embroidered or emblazoned on every clothing article, spend the money for that unique, "Hi, my name is _____" plastic name tag. Your admirers will appreciate it.

7. *Plastic copper bracelet.* You're not after wealth, so don't look as if you are. A dramatic ethnic bracelet or simple "squaw" bangle makes you belong to the entire world.

8. *Mug.* Carry a personalized one with you everywhere. Try a "Go team" mug to show you want to be a team player or want to play with the team.

9. *Jean skirt.* Garlic girls, you are the only ones who can carry off this kind of rugged but rustling skirt. It goes with everything in your wardrobe for work or play. If you're feeling more feminime, sew a ruffle round the edge or top off with a bright colored corduroy seam.

10. *Spot.* You always have one somewhere, no matter how well groomed. It's kind of lovable and makes you more approachable.

11. *Down parka.* Whether it's 90 degrees below or 90 degrees above, you're ready to play. Be sure it's in one of your Garlic Palette colors *(See page 49.)* so it goes with everything else you own.

12. *Large, multi-compartmented handbag.* You've just got to have one that holds all the things you carry around· big hairbrush, barrettes, bobby pins, rubber bands, diaphragm, address book stretched with the names of friends, balled-up kleenexes, shopping lists, checkbook, wadded dollar bills (you're too busy to put in your wallet), a deflated balloon from the last party.

13. *Run.* See #10. The same things hold for runs in your stockings. Actually, you'd rather not even have stockings on, but sometimes society demands it. If you knew you had the run when you put them on, pretend you didn't. No one will call you a liar. Besides, if you remembered to wear a slip, it's showing too, and they'll be distracted by that.

14. *Field hockey stick.* If you really want to accessorize your wardrobe, a hockey stick could be your most personal statement. It shows that you are one of the team and ready to play. Its sleek wood veneer goes with all colors and perfectly coordinates all the active aspects of your Total Garlic Gusto.

15. *Tennis shoes.* Always carry them with you. Who knows when someone will get up a game of something?

16. *Low-heeled, open-toed, open-heeled, almost nothing shoes.* When wearing shoes, these are your best bet. Slip in and out of them with ease, while they protect your feet against any terrain. Get them in one of your palette of Garlic colors.

T.G.G.
The Total
Garlic Gusto...
for men

Garlic Men, you're the *natural* in everything you wear and do. So look that way. Show off your rugged, athletic interior with a wardrobe to match...

1. *100% polyester bold-print shirt.* Shown is a palm tree motif, but any open-collared shirt with a bright vivid pattern is great for showing off your upper torso.

2. *Your chest.* You always know how much hair a Garlic man has on his chest. Reveal what you've got and revel in it. Most Seasonings (except Gingers) will enjoy looking.

3. *Necktie.* Tied in a hurry and picked out in haste...somehow it never goes with any other piece of apparel you have on because you hate ties. Try the lusty colors in your special Garlic Palette. If you have to wear a tie, make it count.

4. *Political button.* You've got opinions and causes. Let the world know about them. Be sure to wear a different one everyday.

5. *A beer.* Like your female counterpart, you've got a taste for the simple pleasures and always like to be feeling good enough to really relish in them. Beer goes particularly well with carry-out pizza and burgers. Leave at least one of these packagings on the floor of the back seat of your car at all times.

6. *Team jacket.* Don't ever be without one...any sport, any school, any service, and any style. It's best when in a two-color combination (again, consult your palette) that defies "good taste." *(See page 49.)*

7. *Full pockets.* We don't hazard a guess as to what's in these. Fill them with goodies. You shouldn't be flat anywhere.

8. *Stain.* Just like your lady, you've got one. We're charmed by it and surmise that even you don't remember what dripped here.

9. *Jock strap.* This man makes no artificial display to show off or hide his essential animal attributes.

10. *The t-shirt.* Let it hang out. It's your uniform. A clean one, worn as an outer garment, will take you from palace to pigsty in equal style.

11. **Gym bag.** Like the feminine hockey stick, it's your badge and serves equally well as your brief case, lunch box, and sporty bag.

12. *No socks*...good heavens, no.

13. *Old loafers or old topsiders.* To a Garlic, there's no such thing as new and shiny, but never try to resole or reheel them, just beat up a new pair.

NOT SHOWN: underwear because it's nonexistent.

Go for it, Garlic!

T.G.S.
The Total
Ginger Standard...
for women

EMILY DICKENSON
SYLVIA PLATH
D.H. LAWRENCE

Ginger women are the staunch individualists of this world, classic and subtle, clever and quiet. Each piece, each element in her wardrobe should generate respect and practicality. The Ginger woman is smart in everything she does.

1. *Long hair wrapped tightly in buns, braids.* You can really let it all hang down, but only in private. In public, your hair is all business, neat and pulled away from your inquiring eyes.

2. *Pearl earrings.* Never wear anything else. These are small, classic, and expensive. They'll never distract you from the task at hand, just add a tiny glitter.

3. *Tie.* The Ginger woman is bound to succeed. This tie, though tidily tied, is feminine but strong.

4. *Sweater chain.* No garment should flop in your way, so hold it neatly in place with this tiny restraint.

5. *Tailored, tucked blouse.* A quiet statement of elegance, this coordinate is trim, and its tiny numerous buttons are unthinkable to more unseemly Seasonings.

6. *Glasses chain.* Ditto for this elegant reminder that glasses are to be worn, not displayed. Besides, you should always be prepared for whatever reading matter comes your way.

7. *Elbow patches.* Why waste a good sweater? Start it out with good leather patches and you'll never be embarrassed by a hole.

8. *Classic leather belt.* In one of your strong neutrals, this belt goes with practically anything.

9. *Bookmark.* Just as the hockey stick is the ultimate Garlic accessory, the bookmark is yours. Make sure it is a fine fringed leather type.

10. *Book.* Goes with everything in your wardrobe and keeps you from being bored, no matter how long you have to wait for success.

11. *Neat, tailored leather shoulder bag.* Sits staunchly on your shoulder and holds only the necessities: comb, eyeglass repair kit, lipstick and blusher for quick repairs, classic leather wallet and tidy, personalized kleenex pouch.

12. *Pleated, tartan skirt or kilt.* It's full of the colors you like best *(See page 49.)* and goes with every blouse you own. It's not too straight for a vigorous walk nor so full that it gives you the "flouncy" look you despise.

13. *Instrument case.* Even if you can't play a single note, look as if you can and do.

14. *Knee socks.* Why risk an embarrassing run? These good socks are warm and colorful and ready for whatever elements you might meet. Turn them down gently under the knee for a tiny extra flair. Wear a little rubberband under the fold to make sure they don't fall down in public.

15. *Good sturdy shoes.* Your feet were meant for walking. Don't risk uncomfortable shoes. These excellent quality leather moccasins never wear out and always look good. You might try a basic black or brown pump for a little dressier look.

16. *Extra reading matter.* Always be prepared. You just might finish one book and have to speak to people around you out of sheer boredom. Be sure the titles are weighty and impressive and always in your field of endeavor, be it poetry or archaeology. You might want to add a small leatherbound notebook and good gold pen for taking notes.

17. *Extra totebag.* Of course, we know you can't fit all those books in that little bag we've given you, so carry this totebag to keep everything in its place. It should have a good strong brass or gold clasp to keep its contents out-of-view. You can hide a "racier" book in its depths, too, like that little field guide to nature.

Ginger feet keep walking, comfortably and correctly.

T.G.S.
The Total
Ginger Standard...
for men

Ginger men are the understated ideal, studied in every garment. In a world of vulgarity, you stand out because of the care you take not to stand out. It's your individuality of mind that shines, not your wardrobe. Keep it simple.

1. Neat expensive haircut. Only the best barber touches your precious locks. He works at making every hair stay in place. The essential element here is that there is NOTHING UNIQUE about the style. It's purely appropriate.

2. Mustache. Constantly trimmed.

3. Button-down shirt and tie bar. Nothing has been left to come undone or to embarrass you. Try one of your Ginger Palette colors in oxford cloth. *(See page 49.)*

4. Rep tie. Any *small* figure is appropriate as long as it refers to your ancestry, your honored society, your gentlemen's sport, or any of the above you wish you had.

5, 6. LEFT: *Chess tournament lapel pin;* RIGHT: *fraternity or professional society pin.* This is often the extent of Ginger jewelry. It always refers to intellectual attachment, or achievement.

7. Navy blue blazer. Gray flannel or camel is equally acceptable.

8. English driving hat. Other seasonings might dare to call it a cabbie hat; but we know better, Gingers, don't we? Perfect for popping into one's Volvo.

9. Suspenders. Always trustworthy.

10. Audi key ring. Any ugly, expensive car will do: Volvo, BMW, Citroen. No one else can appreciate them as you do.

11. Button fly . . . means you really have to ponder your every move before you do it, or undo it.

12. Pleated pants. Always neat and hides everything beneath.

13. 100% cotton starched khaki pants with cuffs . . . go with the pleats above for guaranteed perfection in any casual situation.

14. Non-jug wine. You know the obscure chateaux by name or simply know enough to choose impressive looking labels on sight.

15. Wing tips. Still the gentleman's shoes, but you might try cordovans in brown or black for a simple change.

16. Over-the-calf socks. They may be carefully mended, but no one will ever know. Certainly there are no hairy calves peeping out uninvited.

NOT SHOWN: White cotton boxer undershorts, precisely ironed.

A Gingery arrangement and assortment of the few things admitted into his well groomed wardrobe

Chapter Twelve

The Garden of Herbal Delights

*A Field Guide to Identifying the Seasonings
Right on their own Turf*

The best place to practice identifying the Seasonings is to visit the garden plot of seedling herbs, struggling to assert themselves—suburbia. Starting with the same basic home ground, watch how each Seasoning has added his or her personality.

The Prototype

Living Parsley

Key

1. A clean, full bird bath in a garden planted just like the one on the front of the Burpee catalog—your know the one, where the tulips are set all in rows.

2. The early American lamp post. Electric, usually black with frosted glass. House number on crossbar and rustic wheel are optional features.

3. Brick walk. The concrete one just didn't seem like home.

4. Split-rail fence. This is not hand-hewn but bought at the lumberteria in sections, put up in a single weekend.

5. Mother hen and chicks. Mama Hen has the family name emblazoned on her. Chickies are blank or have one numeral of the house number on each. Piggies, lambs and ducks will also suffice.

6. Birdhouse. An attractive one for our friends with feathers.

7. Window treatment. Look for cafe ruffled curtains. White, pink, and sunshine yellow are preferred colors. Collectibles are lined up on the window frames and can be seen from the outside. Acceptable collections include small pitchers, bud vases, egg cups, ceramic birds, glass horses or penguins, anything little and cute.

8. Woodpile. Parsleys do not buy firewood a few sticks at a time. They get it by the cord so there will always be plenty to toasty-up the family room for the evenings by the hearth.

9. Window boxes. Reminiscent of a cottage in the country. Petunias and French Dwarf marigolds are the standard species of choice.

10. Door frame and balustrade. Just like Mt. Vernon with coach lamps to match the lamp post.

11. Storm door. White enameled metal, the most tasteful all-weather metal Sears has to offer.

12. Geometricallly trimmed shrubbery. Spheres, cones, boxes, and ovoids.

13. Bird feeder. These people *really* like those little critters.

14. Station wagon. How else are you going to transport the entire Brownie troop to roller skating and ice cream cones?

15. Garage turned into a family room with bay window. "Why should we waste the space on the car when Penny and Woody want a Ping-Pong table?"

16. Weather vane. Rustic, rural Americana, wild game, or barnyard themes.

The Pepper Experience

Key

1. **Bronze modern sculpture.**

2. **Floodlights directed on the house at night.** For that focal point the house needs—twenty-four hours a day.

3. **Fountains.** A quiet fish pond does not count; it has to be shooting water, and it has to be out front.

4. **Solid walls and real gates.** Just as the apron on a theater's stage defines the territory of the actors from the territory of the audience, a good wall lets you know that ''some people are inside, and others are most decidely out.''

5. **Gravel between the sidewalk and street.** Never worry about whether anyone is ruining the grass (and you won't have to spend valuable time tending it).

6. **Clean, shiny, late model expensive car.** This alone is not enough to classify someone as a Pepper, but it is absolutely mandatory if you are truly one.

7. **Entrance ornaments.** Defines processional path for those who enter. The bigger the better.

8. **High hedges.** Dense, tight, and often thorned. If Peppers want others to know what goes on inside, they will invite them in.

10 **Sentinels.** Ceramic or stone. Dobermans, greyhounds, Fu dogs, and afghans preferred.

11. **Big windows.** The perfect screen for activities the Peppers want you to see.

12. **Big house numbers.** For new, first-time party guests.

13. **Pylon fiberglass, emblazoned ''CIAO.''**

14. **Pool entrance.** If there is a pool in there, it is either indoors or at least an in-the-ground kidney shaped type. Then again, there may be no pool at all, only the impressive sign.

15. **Dramatic new roof.** It may be black, it may be hot turquoise, but it sure is different from everyone else's in the neighborhood.

16. **Pruned mature trees.** Other Seasonings only prune plants their own size.

BEING
Garlic

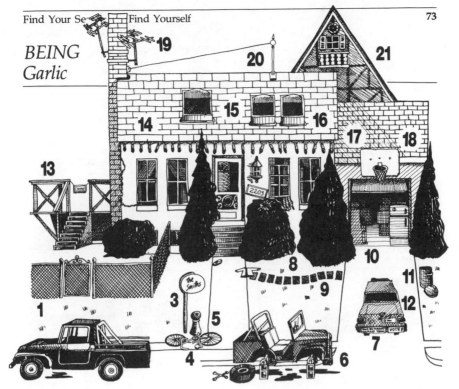

Key

1. Chain–link fence. What more can you say?

3. Name posts. They want you to know who they are and where they live.

4. Spontaneous storage. Bicycles, sporting equipment, and lawn care implements appear in the most unexpected places.

5. Mirrored ball on pedestal. Like the Parsley's birdbath, but less functional. Also would include any sculptural figures or animals or people that are painted. Drunks leaning against lamp posts, flamingos or donkeys pulling carts are other possible choices.

6. Jeeps. Jeeps are really the epitome of Garlic transport. A jeep up on blocks is the cool whip on the Jello.

7. Bumper stickers. "Have you hugged your kid today?" Happy faces. Anti-nuclear, braking for anything, pro everything...Garlics have feelings on all sorts of topics and want you to know they do.

8. Orginal bushes. Overgrown, died off, and never replaced.

9. Flagstones. So quick, so easy...the builder should have put a walk across here, since it's the way we always walk.

10. Full garage. Door left open to expose it.

11. Trash cans left out all the time.

12. Dents and body rust. So long as it's running, why should we replace a perfectly good car? (Note: look for items hanging from rear view mirror.)

13. Above-ground swimming pool. Awkward to sit by but lots of fun in the water.

14. Christmas lights...left up all year. Dead Christmas tree (decorated with cranberries for the birds) still standing in side yard.

15. Skylights. Let the sun shine in on all the happy hanging plants.

16. Basketball net out front so the whole neighborhood can use it.

17. Original roof. Patched. Garlics don't *want* the roof to leak, it just does, that's all.

18. Storm door. Aluminum, metalic finish, initialed, and scrolled.

19. Antennas. More than one...but still they get terrible reception.

20. Science project! Benjamin Franklin and the lightning rod, left up since 1972.

21. Addition in different architectural style. Swiss chalet, country barn, ski lodge, Japanese modern, California casual all preferred to existing Colonial structure.

The Ginger Understatement

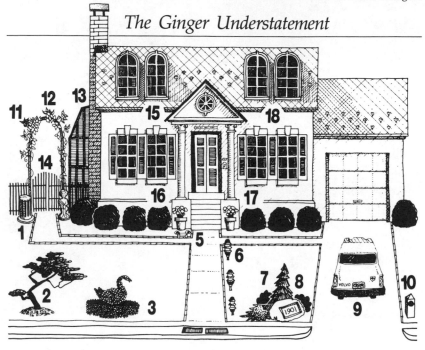

Key

1. Cast-marble-look neoclassical decorations. Broken columns, Putti, numphs, figurative representations of the seasons, Pan, urns, or capitals are the most common. The best ones are from Italy and made of cement but have been slightly chiseled on the surface to look really antique and authentic.

2/3. Highly pruned small trees and topiary. That bonsai look is just perfect. Look for junipers and red maples; and NO ONE but a Ginger would have the patience to attempt a topiary.

5. Flowers in pots in season. Hothouse flowers by the door. Pots should be a natural material and, when in terra cotta, are often tied with grosgrain ribbon.

6. Lamps by the walk. Very functional and in good taste.

7. Small gardens of specimen plants. Dwarf evergreens, Oriental grasses, difficult to grow exotics.

8. House number in stone. Chiseled artistically on a boulder.

9. Four-year-old Volvo. Other styles are acceptable if the country of origin builds machines of the most precise quality.

10. Reflector posts. These give definition and let the world know that they better not step on that grass.

11. Arbor. If you thought this was a trellis, you were mistaken.

12. Wisteria. Perfectly pruned. If you have never had wisteria, you do not know what an accomplishment this is. For any other Seasoning, this stuff would look like Georgia kudzu in no time.

13. Greenhouse. A working, clean, and orderly greenhouse is a Ginger dream. It is nature under control with a gas heater.

14. Wrought-iron fence and gate. The most expensive per foot of all fencing is always correct—and lasts forever.

15. Front porch in the manner of a Roman temple. Compare the proportions to page 130, illustration No. 200 in your copy of Janson's History of Art.

16. Boxwoods. Who else would plant bushes that take thirty years to grow?

17. Small signs by the front door. Can be the last name on a brass plate, a quotation, motto in a foreign language, "Deliveries in rear" or "No Solicitations."

18. Snow cleats in a slate roof. Snow cleats are absolutely unnecessary unless you get more than two feet of snow at a time. But they are that finishing touch—that look of preparedness—that a Ginger strives for.

Now, paste a picture of your house here. Study what you have done to it, the little touches you've added. If you haven't been happy there, perhaps you need more of your seasonal accoutrements.

If you're a Ginger, add that chiseled boulder.
If you're a Parsley, try some regimented tulips.
A Pepper might just need that "Pool Entrance" sign.
And, a Garlic might just need some more bumper stickers
  to complete the look.

Try these hints. You'll find your home becoming more and more your place of comfort and delight.

PASTE
PHOTO
HERE

Chapter Thirteen

Home Fix-It

A Saturday Project for Every Seasoning

Here you have it—a Saturday project for every man and woman of every Seasoning. Never again will you have that uncertain feeling of having time on your hands and nothing to do.

The Parsley Woman

Spruce up your kitchen with a floral counter-top appliance cover. From only two and one half yards of your choice of darling chintz (or an odd, permanent-press sheet), your kitchen will be brightened. It's a household salvation! It covers all those essential household wonders you have squirreled on every possible surface of your kitchen counter.

Toaster Cover

Make a matching potholder while you are at it.

Tri-corner hat from gray felt

Hair made out yarn
Button eyes
Cheeks-spot of red dye
Cross-stitch happy face
Ruffles at the neck
Puff sleeves
Chintz, darling print

Gros grain ribbon
Ruffles at the wrist

Toaster;

or you can put cover over food processor, or half gallon of liquor you want to leave out but not have seen.

Use in bathroom over toilet paper.

OTHER DESIGNS: Poodle, Snowman, etc....

The Parsley Man

Decorate your pet's sleeping quarters. You'll rest assured he (or she) will always get a good night's sleep and be in the best of moods. Imagine the sweet dreams you'll have knowing that your little prince (or princess!) is all snuggy-cozy and comfy-warm.

The Pepper Woman

Organize your clothes by designer label or manufacturer or style. Get EVERYTHING out. First, organize by country, then by individual. *They* design it by grouping; you can now store it that way. If you are heavily into one particular fashion article, divide your apparel into "early," "middle," and "recent," subcatagories. By no means are you required to wear it this way, *mais non;* but it does give respect where respect is due.

ITEM	STYLE/ DESIGNER/ MFG.	DESCRIPTION	GOES WITH
TURQUISE BOOTS	BALLY	Turquoise, chrome studs - medium heels	EVERY-THING
CAPE	From Penneys, but now has St. Laurent Label in it.	RED- WET Look, FULL LENGTH	EVERY-THING
BOA	Mr. Frederick	9 FOOT, white FEATHERS	EVERY-THING
BLOUSE	BILL BLASS	CERISE SILK LOW CUT FRONT, BACK-LESS	EVERY-THING
BAG	FENDI Copy	DISCO BAG,	EVERY-THING
SKIRT	CHANEL LOOK-ALIKE	NAVY WOOL, VERY deep SLITS!	EVERY-THING

① Fill out cards like this for all your clothes and accessories. You may want to have a separate card for each catagory. Post all cards on inside of your closet door

② Make rings for your closet pole to devide clothes by designer.

The Pepper Man

Clean your swimming pool. Go out back. Take off your terry cloth robe. If it is sunny, put on your sunglasses; but put on your sun block no matter what the weather. Set up the chaise longue. Check the water temperature. Turn the pool on automatic-clean. Now, jog around the pool, stopping for ten push-ups, and twenty sit-ups every ten laps.

The Garlic Woman

Put on a big pot of Chili! Follow the enclosed recipe (serves twenty-four, no problem) and you'll have the house full of the aroma that made Carmen Miranda a star before she ever wore that banana headdress. Have the entire neighborhood *in* your kitchen *begging* for the recipe. Relax! Just put on a pot of coffee, give them all a sample, and let the compliments roll in.

Recipe for Chili

In a large skillet, heat
  2 cups salad oil
when the oil is hot, add
   10 medium sliced onions
   10 pounds ground beef
   2 heads (12-14 cloves) garlic, minced

Cook for a few minutes and then add
  five 32 oz. cans of red kidney beans
  1¼ gallons of stewed tomatoes
  ¾ cup paprika   ½ cup brown sugar
  ¾ cup chili powder
  ¼ cup salt   2 T. cayenne pepper

Simmer for 3 hours, stir with golf club or polo mallet.

The Garlic Man

Presto! An armchair holder for BOTH your can of beer *and* the TV remote control. You can actually make this lifesaver with a butcher knife from an old cardboard box. *So simple!* Make it during any halftime or a long commercial break. However, don't rush, you'll have time to make it to the bathroom before the game resumes.

1. Get a nice cardboard box at the Grocery Store.

2. Mark a ½ circle on both ends and lines on the bottom.

3. Cut along dotted line with a butcher knife. Be careful.

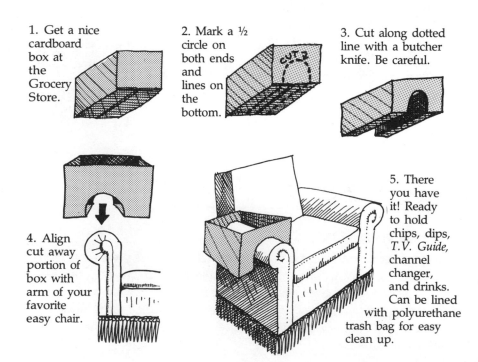

4. Align cut away portion of box with arm of your favorite easy chair.

5. There you have it! Ready to hold chips, dips, *T.V. Guide,* channel changer, and drinks. Can be lined with polyurethane trash bag for easy clean up.

The Ginger Woman

Alphabetize your books by author. Make a card catalog by subject. It's an investment in your future that will save you *hours* in the long run. Imagine: a dozen of your most respected peers are at *your* house after the theater. A heated discussion ensues, and the key issue hangs on the EXACT wording of a quote by Shelley. You stride to the shelf. M, N, O, P, Q, R, S—Sandridge, SHELLEY! (Refresher on the Dewey Decimal System available at your local library.)

The Ginger Man

Clean your kitchen with a toothbrush. You've been thinking about getting behind the knobs on the stove anyway. Looked *under* the bottom of the refrigerator door lately? Have you taken the ear and mouth parts of the telephone receiver apart recently? We knew it...they all need cleaning! Once you start, you'll find *DOZENS* of other hideaways for reclusive (and elusive!) grime. (List of the best grease-cutters available from the Department of Agriculture.)

An exciting Saturday morning with Robert Hickey, Hp.D., a *Ginger*, as he delights in dissecting and polishing the phone, scraping the untidy underside of the faucet, and scrubbing that unsightly garbage disposal under the sink.

Chapter Fourteen

Seasonings Meetings

Love...the Blending of the Spices

Love...that's what the blending of spices is all about. A small dose
of one bad combination can ruin your recipe for a splendid social
affair. But, you might well need the entire dumpster of a good combination to get your pot to a rolling boil.

Let's learn how to mix spices. Study the descriptions of eight spicy
buds (a guy and a gal of each seasoning). Then take the quiz. You'll
be able to see how accurate you are by checking the chart at the
end of the chapter.

Never Ask "What's Your Sign" Again

Having difficulties getting a conversation going with someone
you like? Here are some hints. Just look under the Seasoning
you think your honey is, then root into these subject areas...

	Parsley	*Pepper*	*Garlic*	*Ginger*
Favorite Song	"Climb Every Mountain"	"The Night They Invented Champagne"	"100 Bottles of Beer on the Wall"	Classical, progressive jazz, or try a German *lied*.
Favorite Car	Ford Pinto Station Wagon	Cadillac	Cherokee Chief	1981 Volvo
Favorite Vacation Spot	Rustic mountain lake cabin	Chalet in Zermatt	RV camp site outside Wildwood, N.J.	Viola da gamba festival at local university
Favorite Book	Heidi	Winning through Intimidation	The Joy of Sex	Robert's Rules of Order

☐ Parsley   ☐ Pepper   ☐ Garlic   ☐ Ginger   ☐ Parsley   ☐ Pepper   ☐ Garlic   ☐ Ginger

Penny Royal

Penny was always her mother's pride and joy. She was the toddler with perfect manners and a perfect potty habit. She began organizing her toys in boxes when she was two. She could tie her own hair ribbons when she was five. Penny was that lovely little flower at whom muddy-kneed kids threw ginko nuts.

When Penny hit high school she discovered how cute boys could be. She waited for the phone to ring with calls, and when they came, dating began. Bowling! Meeting after Church! Saturday afternoon movies! Penny soon discovered the key to devotion; brownies for her steady.

Penny went off to college with cute pastel sweaters, ruffled blouses, dreams of romance, and a promise to her parents to have fun, be good and finish school before getting married.

At college came the great crisis. How could she protect her maidenhood? She had promised herself to remain a virgin until she fell in love and got married. For, despite all the struggles for liberation of her fellow women, Penny wanted nothing more than to be a good wife and mother.

Timothy Mugwort

Tim's dorm room is neat; shoes in rows, and coats hung up. He spends Saturday mornings at the library, then plays tennis with his best friends. Like his dad, Tim keeps his hair trimmed, wears crisp white shirts and khaki pants. There's no ring around the collar on this guy.

Now that he's in college, he sees his grandmother all the time. She lives two blocks off campus. He goes over to study in the evenings and to help her with chores.

Tim had a girlfriend. The daughter of his parent's best friend, Pokey used to smile at him while their families had dinner together. They had kissed and held hands, and Tim knew that it would take a long time to get that far with a girl again.

Now he just looks at all the co-eds and wonders how he could ever get to know them. Athough he'd like to be a devil-may-care, "Four F" stud, Tim wants to become very good friends with someone before anything gets out of hand.

☐ Parsley   ☐ Pepper   ☐ Garlic   ☐ Ginger   ☐ Parsley   ☐ Pepper   ☐ Garlic   ☐ Ginger

Lily Burnet

Lily has five brothers. Theirs was a house where a million kids were always running in and out. There was never a reason to bend over to pick up food you might drop on the floor in the kitchen...one of her retrievers, huskies, or brothers would get it first.

As the neighborhood's best tree climber, Lily was completely crushed to learn she was NOT a boy!

Thriving in the pillow fights, wrestling matches, and bathroom lines, she was perfectly prepared for dorm life. Once the most popular Bluebird and kickball champion, she is now the floor president in the sorority house.

Lily is sturdy, firm, and fully packed. Not fat (yet) she looks her absolute best *right this minute*.

A sociology major, Lily has no conception of what she wants to do with her degree. She has read about life as a political campaign worker, (maybe she'll work on Capitol Hill) or as a teacher for retarded children. Both sound good.

Lily doesn't have a boyfriend right now and does she ever miss it! She would never go all the way with someone she didn't love but, fortunately, she falls in love very fast.

Roman Alecost

Roman was the first in his elementary school to have a frog, a boa constrictor, and a Playboy centerfold in his locker, *all* at the same time. He could always get guys together for touch football, and now he is tackle on the Varsity football team.

A's in Phys. Ed. are balanced against C's in French and Geometry. His teachers complain, but at home it's O.K., because his dad did it just the same way. He isn't dumb, he just doesn't study. But honor roll or no honor roll, Roman will be invited to a dozen graduation parties. He is already looking forward to the class reunions.

Roman knows every girl at school with "big ones" by name. There are even certain women for whom he arranges his schedule so he can walk behind them as they go upstairs. He had a high school sweetheart, but that broke off awhile ago. Now he mainly talks about "being crazy" for this one in the tight blouse, or "being hot" for that one in the clinging sweater.

☐ Parsley ☐ Pepper ☐ Garlic ☐ Ginger

☐ Parsley ☐ Pepper ☐ Garlic ☐ Ginger

Viola Henbane

Tall, thin, and flat chested, Viola is poetry editor of the literary magazine. Her own poems usually have complex rhyming patterns that are the delight of the English faculty. Behind those glasses, Viola has large brown eyes that have a striking aura of sophistication. But other than that, she is pretty ordinary looking in her turtlenecks and tweed skirts.

Viola has several good girlfriends, each of whom dreams of achieving success in one field or another; writing law, science, or public service. For Viola, it is to be published before she is thirty.

She wants a perfect romance, too, but so far it seems unlikely to happen with any of the nerds at this school. None of them has that smoldering passion she has read about. So, for now, she is willing to keep her passion under wraps and let it explode later.

Munstead Lovage

In addition to his clothes, Munstead carried his art supplies, thesaurus, and bathroom scales to college. His freshman roommate greeted him with a Budweiser and called him "Mun." "My name is Munstead and I don't drink directly out of cans," was his first spoken reply.

He had lots to learn about living with humanity en masse. Munstead had never seen guys spray gamey underwear with deodorant and put it on again. He, was unaccustomed to toilet stalls without doors. He didn't realize most regular guys drank *only* Coke and didn't drink the Teem or Orange Soda out of the drink machines.

But, Munstead learned quickly. Soon he was accepted and known for his talents. A methodical art major who spent much of his time in the studio painting, he had a secret fantasy he thought about a lot: he wanted to be smarter and more talented than anyone else.

Munstead is, shall we say, sexually inexperienced. He tries to sound knowledgeable in late-night bull sessions, but his knowledge is derived from reading every magazine and sex manual he can get his hands on. He would like a steady, but isn't sure how you go about breaking the ice of campus passion.

☐ Parsley ☐ Pepper ☐ Garlic ☐ Ginger   ☐ Parsley ☐ Pepper ☐ Garlic ☐ Ginger

Cicely Goldthread

An absolute firecracker, Cicely could keep time to the music in her nursery before she was two. Now prima ballerina of the college company, she'll try out for the New York City Ballet as soon as she graduates. Cicely is already willing to practice twelve hours a day to be the prima there, too. Cicely will not fail.

She can wear a burlap sack and make it look sexy, daring, and dangerous. But burlap isn't her style. Cicely pampers her body in cashmere by day or in bubbles by night after her torturous daily workouts.

Cicely lost her virginity at fourteen and never missed it. She attracts lovers the way honey attracts bees. But they don't really captivate her imagination. One is too short. The next has no background. Another has no future. She dreams of her perfect man but knows she hasn't met him yet. So, when she needs a date, she asks out whom *she* wants (discreetly, of course). These local guys will have to do until she meets some real men.

Ransom Dittany

''Wild and Hot Handsome Ransom'' gives the best parties at his off-campus apartment. He decides who are the best party people, then mixes and matches until the evening becomes electric.

He starred in the last college play and is going to spend the summer in a small (but significant) part off-Broadway. With his gleaming good looks and flashing smile, he may try Hollywood after college, just for the money. But Ransom hasn't really decided whether he wants a great acting career or a stellar part in international diplomacy.

Ransom is the most noticed man on campus. No one can dress the way he can. No one can look poured into a pair of jeans the way he can. No one can make a white shirt and a crookedly tied red necktie look so dashing. He titilates every woman on campus, but has usually alighted on each only for the minimum number of passionate minutes.

The Find-a-Lover Game

Now, take the quiz that follows using your knowledge and instinct. Read the descriptions of the situations very carefully. Then choose the correct answer from the choices that follow. An explanation of the correct answer appears at the end of each scenario.

Penny and the Moment of Truth

Penny and a girlfriend go to the Mistletoe Ball. She has been looking forward to this night for a long time. It was going to be a chance to wear the pink prairie granny dress she made for her cousin's wedding. At the dance, she sees Ransom. He looks back at her with a longing look. Her heart is aflutter all evening. She is so enamored she loses count of the cups of delicious wine punch she drinks. The dance over, she goes to get her coat. Approaching from behind, Ransom whispers in her ear, "Let me take you away from all this." And, as if in a dream, he sweeps her away with him in his yellow sports car. Penny finds herself at Ransom's apartment. What will happen next?

1. A long night of passion, lust, and love. Just for a laugh, she wears his athletic supporter as a chin guard and ends up taking it home as a souvenir. It is a big hit back at the dorm, and she hangs it over her door as a trophy.

2. She enjoys Ransom the whole night through. Kissing him on the forehead, and patting him on the fanny as she heads out the door the next morning, she jogs ten miles and feels very satisfied.

3. She lets Ransom kiss her until he is mad with desire. Then she screams and runs out of the apartment. What a close call!

Answer

Penny is a Parsley. Although she does not doubt for an instant that Ransom is a very nice boy, SOMETHING tells her he *MAY NOT* be as pure as she would hope. Realizing this, she does the only thing she can do—she screams.

Ransom is a Pepper. Although momentarily angered at her reaction, he thinks that, if the girl had a bit more sense, she would have been grateful. He realizes he really should have known better. Ransom had never taken anyone home who wore braces and a retainer with her formal gown before. He'd tire of Wendy, Penny, Ginney, or whatever her name was very quickly.

The Correct answer is 3.

*Iambic
Pentameter
Meets
Free Verse*

Viola has written her first play, a haiku melodrama. Entitled "Shattered Muffin," it is being produced by the college repertory company. Tim, in a conscious attempt to "do something different" with himself, lands a small part in the play, that of the Narrow Bench. He appreciates Viola's intensity and originality. She admires his honesty and innocent masculinity. At the opening night cast party, exhilarated by the success of the play, Viola and Tim find themselves entwined, kissing under the stairs, oblivious to the other party goers.

Then what?

1. Viola confesses that the whole play is a big pile of artificiality. All she has ever wanted is to make one man happy. Tim is shocked. He must have been mistaken about her! He has "found himself" in his characterization in the play and has pledged himself to a life of art.

2. They have one night together, then promptly forget it ever happened.

3. They find that they are deeply moved by their impulsive intimacy. In a daze, they begin a relationship that goes on all semester. It isn't all they had in mind. Viola tires of Tim's dogged devotion and Tim can't understand why she needs so much time to herself.

Answer

Both these young people are afraid of extreme passion, although they are certainly not incapable of healthy sex.

Tim is a Parsley. Tim thinks it is great that Viola writes poetry, but why won't she spend her evenings with him and fix him popcorn? How come she always has to be so intellectual?

Viola is a Ginger. Tim is everything that Viola saw in the beginning; however, she had hoped for a few unexpected signs of depth. If he asks her once more to spend her creative time to go and *be* with him, she thinks she will vomit.

A permanent relationship could work out if she could learn to make time for him. After all, he would provide a nice quiet home for her poetry writing.

The Correct answer is 3.

Lily and Social Psychology 202

Lily frantically collects her texts and notebooks and runs off to the library. There, she begins to study for her Social Psych. exam. She has 2000 pages of required reading to finish before 10:00 a.m. tomorrow. Sitting next to her is Munstead, the art major who is quietly reviewing his notes for the same exam. He has already done all the reading and used two colors of highlighters; yellow for items of primary importance and green for items of secondary importance. They are each very much aware of one another. Considering their characters, what is most likely to happen?

1. Lily will smile sweetly but continue to study. Munstead will honor her need to prepare for the exam. He sees the jam she is in and volunteers to give her all his notes "cause I won't need them anymore tonight."

2. Munstead, being hornier than the third infantry after the Pacific campaign, intentionally drops his pencil under the table, then gets under the table, on his hands and knees, to "investigate." Incensed, Lily yells for the librarian and demands Munstead be arrested.

3. Lily says "to hell!" with her exam and invites Munstead over for a glass of wine. Munstead smiles, and readily agrees. Already finished studying, he finds Lily particularly exciting. They go to her dorm room. He shows her his way of scanning the material and shares his notes. She shows him her way of reducing tension and shares her experience.

Answer

Lily is a Garlic. A physical soul, she'll always choose love over scholarship.

Munstead is a Ginger. He only let passion intrude tonight because he didn't really need to study. If Lily learns to leave Munstead alone while he paints, and he learns to pay enough attention to her, their relationship could prove very stable in the long run.

The Correct answer is 3.

"**A**re you a 'Toilet Paper Changer' or a 'Toilet Paper Squanderer?'" asks Hp.D. Hickey.

"Peppers and Garlics too often run off with the last sheet, stranding Parsleys and Gingers with the empty and naked roll. This simple act of taking the time to refill or not refill is a symbol of the vast differences in the Seasonings' self-defined roles."

Beauty And The Beast: Which Is Which?

Cicely, as star of the ballet company, was asked to create a special terpsicorian work for halftime at the homecoming football game. Cicely has a lightening stroke of imagination! She will include a REAL football player! After agonizing hours watching the team, she chooses Roman for his looks, enthusiasm, and defined musculature. Much to her amazement, he makes a graceful and supportive partner. Their *pas de deux* is a great success. At the celebrations that follow, they find they have much to admire in one another. Hours later, they reenact each step of their beautiful dance "on another level." What happens the next day?

1. They decide to get married right away and run off to a justice of the peace.

2. He gives her his letter sweater and class ring. She is delirious! Never could she have imagined that a hunk of zircon and gold plate could be so precious to a woman who receives it from the prince at her side!

3. Roman is eager to go on and is falling more and more in love. Cicely loves him in her own way, but if she is really honest with herself, she likes the muscles on his torso more than the ones between his ears. He's a sweet guy and probably just the right playmate for her until she graduates.

Answer

Cicely is a Pepper. No one, not even lusty Garlic Roman, will satisfy her for long. After school is over, she'll call him periodically over the years, when her ballet company's tour schedule makes it convenient. Roman would do a lot better with Lily or Penny.

The Correct answer is 3.

Seasonings Meetings

All right, you've explored many ways the Seasonings can mix and blend. Now try your hand at love. Consult the following chart in your love life. Take it on every date with you. It helps to first give your prospective mate the Test in Chapter 2.

The Pairs	The Parsley Woman	The Garlic Woman
The Parsley Man	Long lasting. Other seasonings may consider this boring to the point of being a threat to one's sanity, but to the principals, it is safe and pleasant.	She seduced him and he loved it. However, she didn't know men wore that many layers of white cotton. Sexually satisfying if he gets his rest.
The Garlic Man	The American Dream. Produces children who are active in sports and make their own clothes, but is not a sexual tornado. Thrives in the suburbs. He wanted to leave the wedding reception early, but she was having a great time and wouldn't hear of it!	It is amazing it didn't happen sooner. Sensous and competitive. Can be brief unless they hire a maid. Honeymoons are of less importance since it is going to be nothing new and more of the same.
The Ginger Man	Tedious but tenacious. Often they are mutually devoted and set up matching pedestals, both of which she will dust and polish.	She propositioned him three times before he figured it out. Passionate, but better for an affair than a marriage, unless they make real efforts to get along and make it work.
The Pepper Man	In the long haul, this is impossible. Can occur only in short periods of confinement, in snowed-in ski lodges, or on cruise ships and then, only if she has lots of money. It is known as the Jason and the Golden Fleece.	Brief, volatile, and sexually explosive. He may be threatened if he doesn't have the energy or the equipment she demands.

Seasonings Meetings

A brief guide to your chances of a successful relationship with people of any Seasoning...

The Pairs	The Ginger Woman	The Pepper Woman
The Parsley Man	He may be her only hope. She knows him inside and out and likes him anyway. Intense, longlived, and she'll be well taken care of.	Impossible. The poor man faces the risk of sustaining third degree burns over 75% of his body. For her it is quaint but a waste of time
The Garlic Man	She had to make her mind up, but she figured she needed it and he was eager and healthy looking. Potentially brief, but passionate. Probably not in-tellectually satisfying, but with a little work *(and if she is into it)* this could last.	Almost impossible for a long marriage. But for an affair or a one-night stand, it has volcanic possibilities, which is exactly what they both had in mind.
The Ginger Man	Extremely intense. Apt to breed contempt rather than children. May need their own live-in therapist. Can be great dinner guests if they are speaking.	Just might work. It would help if he has a successful career or a prestige connection.
The Pepper Man	Can work if she has her own career and is not above aiming his spotlight.	Remember the finale of A Chorus Line? Remember Vesuvious? Remember World War II? If you can get an ivita-tion to their house for a cocktail party, GO.

Chapter Fifteen

What Flavor Is Your Parachute?

Career Advice for Every Seasoning

Ready for a career transplant or just getting back in the market? Wondering why you're still growing with your current job or have been unable to find one where you take root? Here are myriads of career choices for you (in your Seasoning, of course).

Match these career suggestions against your own skills, ambitions, and hopes. Look only at those in your own Seasoning. You'll have an unhappy crop failure if you try one of the other Seasoning's jobs.

Parsley Occupations

antique-reproduction funiture maker
boiler tender
cable splicer
carpenter
cement mason
cooperative extension service worker
crafts person
dairy herder
dump truck operator
English muffin baker
Fannie Farmer assembly-line worker
front-end alignment specialist
goatherd
greenskeeper
home economics teacher
Hostess Twinkie wrapper
keypunch operator
librarian
milkmaid
miner
Mormon Tabernacle choir member
oil burner installer
quilter
roofer
tire recapper
tool-and-die maker
tracthouse bricklayer
watchmaker (*Mickey Mouse Watches*)
zoological-park animal feeder

Pepper Occupations

auctioneer
Broadway star
chairman of the board
cheerleader
chief
convention center P.R. person
dance star
festival organizer
funeral director
heart transplant surgeon
Indian chief
king or queen
mayor
Monte Carlo Mafia leader
movie star
opera star

police chief
professional famous personality
president
rock star
star
sword swallower
successful entrepreneur
talk show host or hostess
tap dance instructor
top-notch hairdresser
T.V. gossip columnist
T.V. star
university president
Welcome Wagon Hostess
White House spokesperson

Garlic Occupations

ambulance chaser
bandit
bank cashier
Bovine artificial-insemination
    technician
bowling pin machine mechanic
chiropractor
cosmetologist
dietician
gynecologist
health services administrator
host/hostess for Boy Scout Jamboree
house parent
intimate garment seamstress
locker room towel person

masseuse/masseur
missionary
newspaper reporter
orderly
pedicurist
social worker
proctologist
rehabilitation counselor
respiratory therapist
seismologist
shoe salesperson
veterinarian
urologist
waiter/waitress in chili house
waste-water plant operator

Ginger Occupations

air traffic controller
archaeologist
art gallery curator
artist
black humor writer
bookbinder
bookworm
brain surgeon
central office equipment installer
chamber music choral director
Chinese foot binder
darkroom technician
delinquent accounts solicitor
department store display person

dispensing optician
egg sorter
Egyptologist
electrocardiograph technician
entomologist
food chemist
hermit
interior decorator
pathologist
piano tuner
political commentator
radiologist
symphony conductor
welder

Chapter Sixteen

The Final Quiz

The Bouquet Garni Concept

Now that you've finished reading this book, you should be ready to understand LIFE and all its Seasonings. You should be ready for the ultimate goal: to be a *BOUQUET GARNI*, whatever your Seasoning. What is a Bouquet Garni? It's the person whose perceptions of Life are so subtle and sophisticated, so worldly and wise, that he or she becomes a magic blend of all the Seasonings, able to appreciate and be the best of each.

Think you are ready for this distinction? Then try The Final Quiz. The Quiz is based on the movie, "The Wizard of Oz" because we feel this classic film assimilates all the teachings of herbopsychiatry in one dramatic rendition.

If you score 6 or higher on this Quiz, you can receive a special *"Doctoral Diploma in Herbopsychiatry"* and be entitled to use the initials "Hp.D." after your name, (Doctor of Herbopsychiatry). You'll be the Bouquet Garni, and that's better than any Top Banana. (*More information on the Diploma at the end of the quiz.*)

The Final Quiz: The Wizard of Oz

1. The Scarecrow thought he was a _____, but wanted to be a _____.

2. The Cowardly Lion thought he was a _____, but wanted to be a _____.

3. The Tin Woodsman thought he was a _____, but wanted to be a _____.

4. Glenda, the Good Witch of the North was a _____

5. The Wicked Witch of the East was a bad _____.

6. The Wizard of Oz failed in being the wizard because he was a
_____ trying to be a _____.

7. Dorothy was really a _____.

8. Dorothy discovered she was not a _____
because she discovered that, all she wanted was to return to
Kansas.

9. For Parsleys, "there is no place like _____."

10. The Message of the "The Wizard of Oz" in herbopsychiatric
terms is: "Never try to be a _____
that you are not."

Become an Hp.D.: A Doctor of Herbopsychiatry

After you answer this difficult QUIZ, send it to the address below
(with your check for $5.00 for postage and handling). The authors
will grade your quiz and *if you are entitled to it*, send you your special,
authentic, impressive and absolutely fabulously real *"Doctoral
Diploma in Herbopsychiatry"*. You will know your own Seasoning
and be ready to flavor and savor the Great Stew of Life.

Make your $5.00 check payable to ACROPOLIS BOOKS LTD.
and mail to:

Acropolis Books Ltd.
2400 17th St., N.W.
Washington, D.C. 20009
ATTN: Hickey & Hughes,
        Herbopsychiatric Institute

Index

Bibliography

Eiseman, Leatrice. 1983. *Alive With Color.*
   Washington, D.C.: Acropolis Books, Ltd.
Hummel, Dean and McDaniels, Carl. 1979.
   Unlock Your Child's Potential. Washing-
   ton, D.C.: Acropolis Books, Ltd.
Jackson, Carole. 1980. *Color Me Beautiful.*
   Washington, D.C.: Acropolis Books, Ltd.
Miller, Clare. 1984. *8 Minute Makeovers.*
   Washington, D.C.: Acropolis Books, Ltd.
Lemieux, Jody. 1982. *Diet signs.* Washington,
   D.C.: Acropolis Books, Ltd.
Mitchell, Charlene and Burdick, Thomas. 1983.
   The Extra Edge. Washington, D.C.:
   Acropolis Books, Ltd.
Nickels, William G. 1981. *Win The Happiness
   Game.* Washington, D.C.: Acropolis
   Books, Ltd.
Olds, Ruthanne. 1984. *Big & Beautiful.* Wash-
   ington, D.C.: Acropolis Books, Ltd.
Wallach, Janet. 1981. *Working Wardrobe.*
   Washington, D.C.: Acropolis Books, Ltd.

Photo Prop Credits

Thanks to the following people whose closets
we raided for photo props: Neil Hughes, Sara
Hughes, Jenny Hughes, Mr. & Mrs. Thomas J.
Hickey, Col. & Mrs. Robert B. Neville, Mr. &
Mrs. George Clark, Jane Ann Simpson & Ruf-
fin. Herbopsychiatric Hat (*p. 6*) created by
Rosemary Hickey.

Photo Credits

Thanks to the following Acropolis and Color-
tone Press people who posed for our pictures:
Colleen Holmes, Lisa Yane, Dale Fisher, Eileen
Tansill, Larry Willis, Chuck Durbin, David
Uslan and George Kostas.

Hickey & Hughes
Robert Hickey (*a Ginger*) did his undergraduate work at
The University of Virginia in psychology, and his graduate
work in herbopsychiatry in the real world of publishing.
He has been art director for scores of how-to and self-help
books, and is currently teaching at The George
Washington University.
   Kathleen Hughes (*a Parsley*) did her undergraduate work
at Brown University in American Civilization, and she,
too, did her graduate work in herbopsychiatry in the
world of publishing. She has edited and marketed scores of
how-to and self-help books (including *Color Me Beautiful*).
She is married, of course, and has two daughters.